SUDOKU

CROSSWORDS   WORD SEARCHES

LOGIC PUZZLES   & SURPRISES!

mind
STRETCHERS

VOLUME 6

EDITED BY ALLEN D. BRAGDON

Reader's
digest

New York / Montreal

ISBN 978-1-62145-408-3

Address any comments about *Mind Stretchers, Volume 6* to:

Reader's Digest Adult Trade Books
44 South Broadway
White Plains, NY 10601

Visit us on the Web:
rd.com (in the United States)
readersdigest.ca (in Canada)

Printed in China

10 9 8 7 6 5 4 3 2 1

Contents

Dear Puzzler,

Tongue twisters push the envelope of the rapid, coordinated articulation skills that are a hallmark of human language. These are skills for which females have an edge.

Read the following tongue twisters twice out loud for practice, and then read them out loud, in order, as rapidly as you can. (Watch out for the third one!) Your attempt only counts if you take 25 seconds or less to recite all 5 tongue twisters. Here they are:

- Clean clams crammed in clean cans. How can a clam cram in a clean cream can?
- If Stu chews shoes, should Stu choose the shoes he chews?
- I saw Susie sitting in a shoe shine shop. Where she sits she shines, and where she shines she sits.
- The thirty-three thieves thought that they thrilled the throne throughout Thursday.
- She saw Sheriff's shoes on the sofa. But was she so sure she saw Sheriff's shoes on the sofa?

SCORING

No mistakes—excellent

1–3 mistakes—good

4–5 mistakes—fair

More than 5 mistakes—you probably don't have a future in radio broadcasting!

While it is an interesting challenge and great fun to recite tongue twisters they also have practical applications in increasing verbal agility, especially useful for public speakers, and have also been used in scientific research aimed at understanding how we process language.

Enjoy this edition of *Mind Stretchers*. Don't let the compilers defeat you!

Allen D. Bragdon

Mind Stretchers Puzzle Editor

■ Meet the Authors

Allen D. Bragdon

Allen describes himself as "the whimsical old dog with puzzle experience and a curious mind." He is a member of the Society for Neuroscience, founding editor of *Games* magazine and editor of the Playspace daily puzzle column, formerly syndicated internationally by *The New York Times*. The author of dozens of books of professional and academic examinations and how-to instructions in practical skills, Allen is also the director of the Brainwaves Center.

PeterFrank

PeterFrank was founded in 2000. It is a partnership between High Performance bvba, owned by Peter De Schepper, and Frank Coussement bvba, owned by Frank Coussement. Together they form a dynamic, full-service content provider specialized in media content. They have more than twenty years of experience in publishing management, art/design and software development for newspapers, consumer magazines, special interest publications and new media.

John M. Samson

John M. Samson is currently editor of Simon & Schuster's *Mega Crossword Series*. His crosswords have appeared on cereal boxes, rock album covers, quilts, jigsaw puzzles, posters, advertisements, newspapers, magazines ... and sides of buildings. John also enjoys painting and writing for the stage and screen.

Sam Bellotto Jr.

Sam Bellotto Jr. has been making puzzles professionally since 1979, when he broke into the business by placing his first sale with *The New York Times Magazine* under then crossword puzzle editor Eugene T. Maleska. Sam has been a regular contributor to Simon & Schuster, *The New York Times*, Random House, and magazines such as *Back Stage*, *Central New York*, *Public Citizen* and *Music Alive!* Bellotto's Rochester, NY-based company, Crossdown, develops word-puzzle computer games and crossword construction software.

When Sam is not puzzling he's out hiking with Petra, his black Labrador dog.

BrainSnack®

The internationally registered trademark BrainSnack® stands for challenging, language-independent, logical puzzles and mind games for kids, young adults and adults. The brand stands for high-quality puzzles. Whether they are made by hand, such as visual puzzles, or generated by a computer, such as sudoku, all puzzles are tested by the target group they are made for before they are made available. In order to guarantee that computer-generated puzzles can actually be solved by humans, BrainSnack® makes programs that only use human logic algorithms.

■ Meet the Puzzles

Mind Stretchers is filled with a delightful mix of classic and new puzzle types. To help you get started, here are instructions for each, with tips and examples included.

WORD GAMES

Crossword Puzzles

Clues. Clues. Clues.

    Clues are the deciding factor that determines crossword-solving difficulty. Many solvers mistakenly think strange and unusual words are what make a puzzle challenging. In reality, crossword constructors generally try to avoid grid esoterica, opting for familiar words and expressions.

    For example, here are some actual clues you'll be encountering and their respective difficulty levels:

LEVEL 1	Vijay Singh's homeland
LEVEL 2	*Entourage* character Gold
LEVEL 3	Lake of Japan
LEVEL 4	Adopted son of Claudius
LEVEL 5	Debussy work

    Clues to amuse. Clues to educate. Clues to challenge your mind.

    All the clues are there—what's needed now is your answers.

    Happy solving!

Word Searches
by PeterFrank

Both kids and grown-ups love 'em, making word searches one of the most popular types of puzzle. In a word search, the challenge is to find hidden words within a grid of letters. In the typical puzzle, words can be found in vertical columns, horizontal rows or along diagonals, with the letters of the words running either forward or backward. You'll be given a list of words to find. But it does not stop there. There is a hidden message—related to the theme of the word search—in the letters left behind after all of the clues have been found. String together those extra letters, and the message will reveal itself.

Hints: *One of the most reliable and efficient searching methods is to scan each row from top to bottom for the first letter of the word. So if you are looking for "violin," you would look for the letter "v." When you find one, look at all the letters that surround it for the second letter of the word (in this case, "i"). Each time you find a correct two-letter combination (in this case, "vi"), you can then scan either for the correct three-letter combination ("vio") or the whole word.*

Word Sudoku
by PeterFrank

Sudoku puzzles have become hugely popular, and our word sudoku puzzles bring a much-loved challenge to word puzzlers.

The basic sudoku puzzle is a 9 x 9 square grid, split into 9 square regions, each containing 9 cells. You need to complete the grid so that each row, each column and each 3 x 3 frame contains the nine letters from the black box above the grid.

There is always a hidden nine-letter word in the diagonal from top left to bottom right.

EXAMPLE   **SOLUTION**

NUMBER GAMES

Sudoku

by PeterFrank

The original sudoku number format is amazingly popular the world over due to its simplicity and challenge.

The basic sudoku puzzle is a 9 x 9 square grid, split into 9 square regions, each containing 9 cells. Complete the grid so that each row, each column and each 3 x 3 frame contains every number from 1 to 9.

EXAMPLE   **SOLUTION**

As well as classic sudoku puzzles, you'll also find sudoku X puzzles, where the main diagonals must also include every number from 1 to 9, and sudoku twins with two overlapping grids.

Kakuro

by PeterFrank

These puzzles are like crosswords with numbers. There are clues across and down, but the clues are numbers. The solution is a sum which adds up to the clue number.

Each number in a black area is the sum of the numbers that you have to enter in the empty boxes beside or below. The empty boxes that make up the sum are called a run. The sum of the across run is written above the diagonal in the black area, while the sum of the down run is written below the diagonal.

Runs can contain only the numbers 1 through 9, and each number in a run can only be used once. The gray boxes contain only odd numbers and the white contain only even numbers.

EXAMPLE   **SOLUTION**

LOGIC PUZZLES

Binairo

by PeterFrank

Binairo puzzles look similar to sudoku puzzles. They are just as simple and challenging but that is where the similarity ends.

There are two versions: odd and even. The even puzzles feature a 12 x 12 grid. You need to complete the grid with zeros and ones, until there are 6 zeros and 6 ones in every row and every column. No more than two of the same number can be next to or under each other. Rows or columns with exactly the same combination are not allowed.

EXAMPLE   SOLUTION

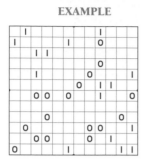

The odd puzzles feature an 11 x 11 grid. You need to complete the grid with zeros and ones until there are 5 zeros and 6 ones in every row and column.

Keep Going

In this puzzle, start on a blank square of your choice and connect as many blank squares as possible with one single continuous line.

You can only connect squares along vertical and horizontal lines, not along diagonals. You must continue the connecting line up until the next obstacle—i.e., the rim of the box, a black square or a square that has already been used.

You can change direction at any obstacle you meet. Each square can be used only once. The number of blank squares left unused is marked in the upper square. There is more than one solution, but we include only one solution in our answer key.

 EXAMPLE   SOLUTION

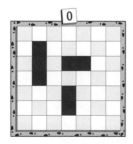   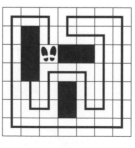

Number Cluster

by PeterFrank

Number Cluster puzzles are language-free, logical numerical problems. They consist of cubes on a 6 x 6 grid. Numbers have been placed in some of the cubes, while the rest are empty. Your challenge is to complete the grid by creating runs of the same number and length as the number supplied. So where a cube with the number 5 has been included on the grid, you need to create a run of five number 5s, including the cube already shown. The run can be horizontal, vertical, or both horizontal and vertical.

EXAMPLE   SOLUTION

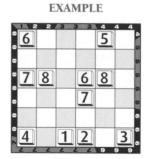

Word Pyramid

Each word in the pyramid has the letters of the word above it, plus a new letter.

Start with the answer to clue No.1 and work your way to the base of the pyramid to complete the word pyramid.

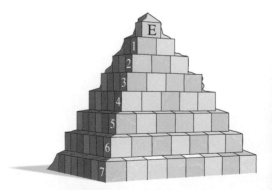

Sport Maze

This puzzle is presented on a 6 x 6 grid. Your starting point is indicated by a red cell with a ball and a number. Your objective is to draw the shortest route from the ball to the goal, the only square without a number. You can only move along vertical and horizontal lines, not along diagonals. The figure on each square indicates the number of squares the ball must be moved in the same direction. You can change direction at each stop.

EXAMPLE   SOLUTION

Cage the Animals

This puzzle presents you with a zoo divided into a 16 x 16 grid. The different animals on the grid need to be separated. Draw lines that will completely divide up the grid into smaller squares, with exactly one animal per square. The squares should not overlap.

EXAMPLE   SOLUTION

Throughout *Mind Stretchers* you will find unique mazes, visual conundrums and other colorful challenges. Each comes with a new name and unique instructions. Our best advice? Patience and perseverance. Your eyes will need time to unravel the visual secrets.

BrainSnack® Puzzles

To solve a BrainSnack® puzzle, you must think logically. You'll need to use one or several strategies to detect direction, differences and/or similarities, associations, calculations, order, spatial insight, colors, quantities and distances. A BrainSnack® ensures that all the brain's capacities are fully engaged. These are brain sports at their best!

Sunny Weather

We all want to know the weather forecast, and here's your chance to figure it out! Arrows are scattered on a grid. Each arrow points toward a space where a sun symbol should be, but the symbols cannot be next to each other vertically, horizontally or diagonally. A symbol cannot be placed on top of an arrow. You must determine where the symbols should be placed.

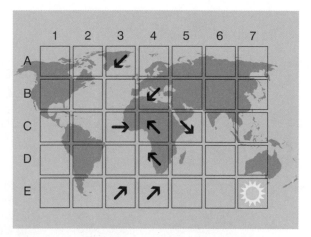

You'll also find more than 100 short brainteasers scattered throughout these pages. These puzzles, found at the bottom of the page, will give you a little light relief from the more intense puzzles while still challenging you.

• ONE LETTER LESS OR MORE

A G E N C I E S -E ☐ ☐ A ☐ ☐ ☐

• LETTERBLOCKS

• BLOCK ANAGRAM

SHADY OIL   *(leisure time away from work)*

☐ ☐ ☐ ☐ ☐ A ☐ ☐

• DOODLE PUZZLE

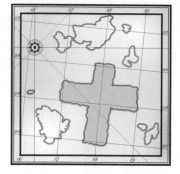

But wait—there's more!

There are additional brainteasers at the top of odd numbered pages, organized into two categories:

• **QUICK!:** These tests challenge your ability to instantly calculate numbers or recall well-known facts.

• **DO YOU KNOW...:** These more demanding questions probe the depth of your knowledge of facts and trivia.

■ Master Class: Spatial Ability and Gender

Are Men Better than Women in Performing Certain Tasks?

No doubt few women appreciate being told that the female brain just isn't designed to handle parallel parking or map reading. But does data actually exist to support the claim that men are better than women at the kinds of spatial intelligence these tasks require?

What do Spatial IQ Questions Really Test?

Psychologists generally believe spatial ability is one kind of intelligence that really does show a gender gap, but the tests that reveal the gap do not involve anything like parallel parking!

When psychologists argue for a biologically based male superiority in spatial intelligence, they are basing their argument on IQ tests that specifically target subtypes of spatial abilities. This is important information if you want to put the gender gap in proper perspective.

Generally, the spatial IQ questions showing the biggest gender differences are in the subcategory known as "mental transformations" or "spatial visualizations." These exercises challenge a person to picture in their mind's eye what an object would look like if it were rotated, viewed from another perspective or folded.

Other questions test what is known as "flexibility of closure" and require the subject to visually "disembed" a shape from a larger, more complex shape, while maze challenges test orientation skill. Tests like these are designed to be pure examinations of spatial abilities. Relying on non-spatial skills, such as verbal skills, to solve spatial challenges may provide a running commentary, but not a solution.

Applying Other Research

There is much research to support at least some biological basis for differences in spatial intelligence between males and females. Animal-based spatial intelligence research, such as maze-running, shows a sex difference—with the superiority lying consistently with the animals whose spatial skills have been altered by manipulating their sex hormones, either before birth or after. Those studies do not prove that human sex differences in spatial intelligence exist or have a biological basis, but they indicate it is unlikely the differences revealed by spatial IQ tests are purely cultural.

Also, human males and females display persistent differences in their brain activation patterns corresponding to spatial tasks. In general, brain activity in men tends to be lateralized toward the right cortex, while women's brains show more bilateral activity. (There is evidence for gender differences in subcortical structures too, in particular the hippocampus.)

Some imaging studies have shown more activation in the parietal lobe of men, compared to in the frontal lobes of women. The right parietal lobe is associated with non-verbal holistic spatial representations, while the frontal lobes are used more generally to solve problems of a variety of types, including verbal problems.

Again, that doesn't prove anything about whether men or women are better at spatial tasks, but it does suggest that different brain activation patterns in men and women may underlie the male edge as measured by spatial IQ tests. Simply put, it may be that more exclusively right-brain-focused activity works better for some visualization skills—and men tend to show that pattern more than women do.

Looking at It From a Different Angle

In everyday life, applications of spatial intelligence involve so many other kinds of intelligence, not to mention practice and training; thus, it is hard to know if tests of "pure" spatial intelligence are, in fact, identifying practical gender differences.

Additionally, almost all researchers agree that the reasons for the male dominance in stereotypically male fields and skills are at least partly cultural, with cultural expectations pushing boys or girls toward or away from certain professions and hobbies.

Most interestingly, there is a persuasive point of view that the male-female differences revealed by spatial IQ tests might be more fairly viewed in terms of differences in cognitive style rather than simple superiority or inferiority.

Brain imaging studies that show more bilateral brain activation for women prove that women do not just use less of their right-hemisphere spatial centers to solve visual puzzles, but that they also use additional brain centers men do not use. Among other things, it may be that women tend to use a more deliberate, verbally-based strategy than men—just as women show a greater verbal orientation in other ways. Men, on the other hand, may use a more exclusively non-verbal strategy, and that difference may result in a greater male quickness in mental visualization tasks, which is essentially what the IQ tests reveal.

Open and Shut Case

Try this exercise. The ingenious partner of a pet store owner constructed the system shown below for opening some, but not all, of the animals' cages. One night he suffered a T.I.A. and now he cannot remember which cages' doors will open and which close when the

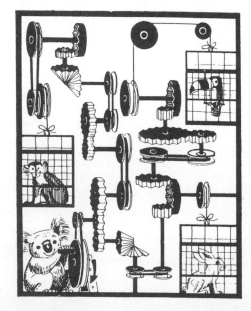

handle is cranked clockwise. Help him out and test the visuospatial circuits of your right brain by following the cogged gears, belted wheels and elliptical gears to the pulleys connected to each cage's door.

The point of this task is this: when the handle is cranked clockwise, predict which cage will open and which will close—the toucan's, the rabbit's or the chimp's. For help, see the HINT below—but try to figure it out first.

The answer is at the end of this Master Class.

Hint: elliptical gears (cone-shaped at right angles) rotate in opposite directions. So, whichever direction one gear turns it will push the attached gear in the opposite direction.

This way of looking at the differences is applicable to a range of spatial skills that show a gender difference. Although the evidence is limited, women seem to show a greater tendency to use landmarks to orient themselves in their environment, or to find their way out of mazes, or through the streets of a strange city. Men seem to rely more on an intrinsic sense of direction. (Indeed, male and female rats display the identical sex difference.) Gender differences in spatial intelligence, then, may result from different choices between two paths that both lead to Rome; one may be quicker, but the other may afford greater enjoyment of the scenery.

Staying with mechanical thoughts of gears and parallel parking, let's move from spatial awareness and look at tactile stimulus. Fingerprints on glossy fenders of cars at an auto show tell the importance of touch in our relationship with the world. To the chagrin of polish-wielding exhibitors, visitors want to touch the cars—run their hands across the paint, open and close doors, and try the seats. Car manufacturers have finally begun to notice. In the past few years, tactile stimulus has become a hot topic. Engineers now spend considerable time on such seemingly mundane issues as the way a compartment or tray closes, how a switch responds and even how paint reacts to touch.

The burgeoning science of haptics (related to the sense of touch) is beginning to tap into a major area of cognitive response. The sensory impact of touch is now being factored into product design and even offers tantalizing clues about the mechanism of one of medicine's most baffling mental illnesses, anorexia nervosa.

Touch Informs Design

As similar products compete in the market place, designers and those involved in marketing seek out novel ways to differentiate them. Innovative uses of touch are now beginning to join sight, sound and smell in their creative quivers. Some examples: yogurt lovers in Switzerland were found to prefer the creamy variety, while the French like theirs lumpy; and for much of the last century, passengers had to push their car door handles in a counter-intuitive direction, that is inward, to get the door to open—only more recently have manufacturers introduced handles that unlatch with an outward tug.

Designing new features into products is taxing the information-conveying ability of already overloaded visual and auditory systems. Proposed steering wheels, that vibrate or heat up in response to a driving hazard, are one such solution. Touch can accurately simulate and transmit sensory data to human users. Computer game manufacturers—who routinely offer controllers some sort of force feedback— are at the forefront of this field, but work proceeds in non-gaming environments as well.

A company named SensAble Technologies has marketed a computer-controlled joystick-like device called Phantom, which allows medical students to simulate unpleasant medical procedures like palpating a prostate without having to fumble on a live patient.

Anorexia: A Window into the Physiology of Touch

Martin Grunwald, a German scientist studying how haptic information is processed and stored, happened upon a discovery that not only advanced the field, but also brought new understanding to the structural dysfunction underlying the medical puzzle of anorexia nervosa. In his experiment, blindfolded subjects were allowed to finger a raised pattern, then asked to draw the pattern on paper. One subject's drawings remarkably bore no relation whatsoever to the tactile pattern. That subject was also anorexic. Further study revealed that, for some reason, anorexia sufferers generally had great difficulty processing tactile sensations. The tactile disconnect persisted in recovered anorexics even after they regained weight, leading Grunwald to suspect that the condition might be related to a common problem in the brain, specifically in the region responsible for touch, the parietal cortex. Grunwald's work with anorexics has also revealed that conscious awareness of touch is not "on" all of the time. Rather, it takes periodic, millisecond-long breaks, a phenomenon that has also been noted with visual stimuli. Some believe that these pauses allow the brain to process or store some of the information it has received.

Design Informs Touch

In the future, haptics research may allow man to extend the limits of his perception, enabling the ability to feel things he has never felt before, or touch something infinitesimally small or thousands of miles away. It may also one day allow the repair of nerve damage that results in neuropathy, or the loss of the sensation of touch. Researchers at M.I.T. recently succeeded in implanting a computer chip in the brain of a monkey which, for reasons of their own, deceived the animal's cognitive systems sufficiently that it felt it was holding a real banana in its hand; a procedure which, on the surface of it, could bode ill for higher primates.

Perhaps, and fortunately, the new science of haptics cannot yet convincingly mimic in humans all the subtleties of even simple tactile sensations. Chief among many obstacles is the sheer complexity of the task. The skin of a human hand alone has 10,000 tactile receptors. Might a future pianist some day be able to play a haptic piano with the range and emotion of Horowitz? Perhaps, but first he should master "Feelings."

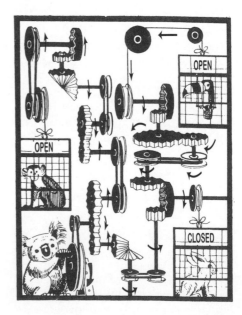

Open and Shut Case Answer
The toucan's and chimp's cages open. The rabbit's closes.

★ By Jiminy! by Cindy Wheeler

ACROSS

1 Young zebra
5 Forelimb bone
9 Muslim headscarf
14 Going nowhere
15 City light
16 Habit
17 *South Park* character
19 Stadium tops
20 More nuts
21 Continuous
23 Wintry chill
24 Auto pioneer Ransom
25 Spurns
29 Less sour
32 Parsley family plant
33 Press and fold, say
35 Thing on a ring
36 Edith Evans, e.g.
37 DeVito in *Hoffa*
38 Kookaburra, e.g.
39 CIRRUS machine
40 Got white with fright
41 Osmond or Antoinette
42 Fabled fox
44 Fore-and-aft sail
46 Was clad in
47 Ampersand's meaning
48 Shaded promenade
51 Laces into
55 Extortionist, e.g.
56 Kermit the Frog's creator
58 Turn away, as one's eyes
59 Five-star Las Vegas hotel
60 Thomas ____ Edison
61 Gets out of bed
62 Biopic about John Reed
63 Flow slow

DOWN

1 Vijay Singh's homeland
2 Chief god of the Aesir
3 Beggar's request
4 Beirut populace
5 Broken, as promises
6 Cartoon wolf's look
7 Word paired with "neither"
8 Prince William's aunt
9 Nestled together
10 Wagner's *Tristan und* ____
11 *Star Trek* hero
12 Iron and Industrial
13 Porgy's lady
18 2011 Belmont winner Ruler ____
22 "Forget about it!"
25 Missile tracker
26 Growing out (of)
27 Wikipedia cofounder
28 Scandinavian poet
29 Wires, in a sense
30 Causing shivers
31 Winona in *Black Swan*
34 Nashville-to-Louisville dir.
37 Defied
38 Large handkerchiefs
40 Curfew setters
41 Clergyman's abode
43 "Uncle!"
45 Titled Turks
48 Quite distantly
49 Big name in jeans
50 Admitting a draft
51 Surrounded by
52 ____ of Wight
53 Word represented by a heart
54 Lose it
57 Anger

★ BrainSnack®—Family Ties

Knowing that their pedigree includes only white and three other colors, which butterfly (A–D) doesn't belong to this family?

CHANGELINGS

Each of the three lines of letters below spell words which are very positive and encouraging, but the letters have been mixed up. Four letters from the first word are now in the third line, four letters from the third word are in the second line and four letters from the second word are in the first line. The remaining letters are in their original places. What are the words?

X R O L U C N I C E
E S C E C L E F U E
P U D C E S S T V L

★ Belgian Beers

All the words are hidden vertically, horizontally or diagonally—in both directions. The letters that remain unused form a sentence from left to right.

```
J L T C A M B R I N U S R J A
U E R P B R I G A N D P I A E
P G O S T B E E R B I S B C U
I E K L L E U Q S L R A K O V
L U C N I K P A H R J A L B E
E R O E W E E D B U Y A B I L
R B B T R N A G L P V P L N L
E O I S T S O I G I M O E S E
I O C N K S U L R U R O V F B
B A E H T S A O L V R H U E O
L E F F E T L R A I D B D E R
E I F F S F O L F T T H E C I
M S E I L T O D E U G N I E T
M E R F R I C R C H I M A Y I
O C O A M N G S T O F T H C E
H S L T M A R E D S O U S R I
C T F O B S N A M E D N I L S
E R V A G R I S E T T E N C E
```

CHIMAY
CRISTAL
DEUGNIET
DUVEL
FLOREFFE
FLORIVAL
GRISETTE
HAPKIN
HOMMELBIER
JACOBINS
JULIUS
JUPILER
KARLSQUELL
LEFFE
LIEFMANS
LINDEMANS
MAREDSOUS
ORVAL
ROCHEFORT

AFFLIGEM
BARBAR
BELLEVUE

BOCKOR
BRIGAND
BRUEGEL

BRUGGE
CAMBRINUS
CANTILLON

DELETE ONE

Delete one letter from NOMINATE and refer to something briefly.

★ ★ George Clooney by Linda Lather

ACROSS

1 Persian monarch
5 Rocky rival Apollo
10 Order
14 Door feature, perhaps
15 Imposing swarm
16 Fabled loser
17 Nick and Nora's pet
18 Out on the waves
19 Big-budget film
20 Where George was Matt King
23 Tennis do-over
24 "Achy Breaky Heart" singer: Init.
25 Earned an Olympic podium spot
29 Bush Supreme Court pick
33 Molecular constituent
34 Blunt or Deschanel
36 "___-hunting we will go ..."
37 Where George was Billy Tyne
41 High hill
42 Alicia Keys hit
43 Banana stalk
44 Perfume
46 Picture puzzles
49 "Disgusting!"
50 Jollity
51 Where George was Mike Morris
59 Feudal estate
60 Ocarina-shaped
61 Lunar sea
62 Stocking shade
63 Derived from wine
64 Dietary supplement
65 Winter air
66 To-be, in politics
67 Bar-tacks

DOWN

1 Soon-forgotten quarrel
2 Corned-beef ___
3 Poker throw-in
4 Miner's light
5 Uncorrupted
6 College military org.
7 Highland language
8 Eve's birthplace
9 It's a lock
10 Question regarding origin
11 More than engaged
12 Purple bloom
13 Sleuth, slangily
21 Slitherer in the water
22 Beefy fast-food chain
25 Dull finish
26 Societal standards
27 They walk the walk
28 Creator of Crusoe
29 Kitchen gadget
30 Origins
31 Magi number
32 Emma in *Supernova*
35 *A Few Good* ___ (1992)
38 World-weary feeling
39 Pigeon
40 Scary waves
45 A lot to see
47 Result
48 Loafer
51 Native Costa Rican
52 Roll response
53 Dastardly doings
54 Compos mentis
55 Of the ear
56 Like the spotted owl
57 Brag
58 *Chicken Run* prisoners
59 Quagmire

★★ Keep Going

Start on a blank square of your choice and connect as many blank squares as possible with one single continuous line. You can only connect squares along vertical and horizontal lines. You must continue the connecting line up until the next obstacle, i.e., the rim of the box, a black square or a square that has already been used. You can change direction at any obstacle you meet. Each square can be used only once. The number of blank squares that will be left unused is marked in the upper square. There is more than one solution. We show only one solution.

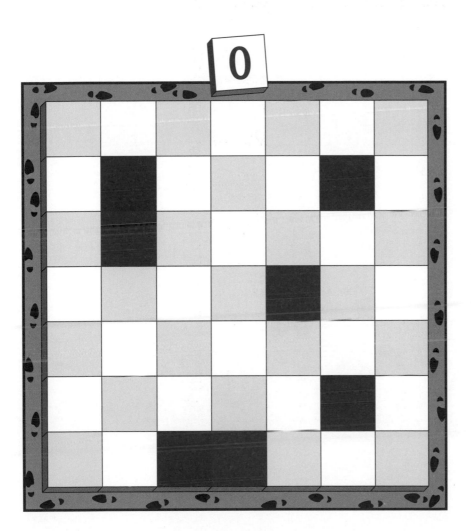

FRIENDS?

What do the following words have in common?

STIMULANT DISTINCTION NATURAL BAND BASS

★★★ Sport Maze

Draw the shortest way from the ball to the goal. You can only move along vertical and horizontal lines, not along diagonal lines. The figure on each square indicates the number of squares the ball must be moved in the same direction. You can change direction at each stop.

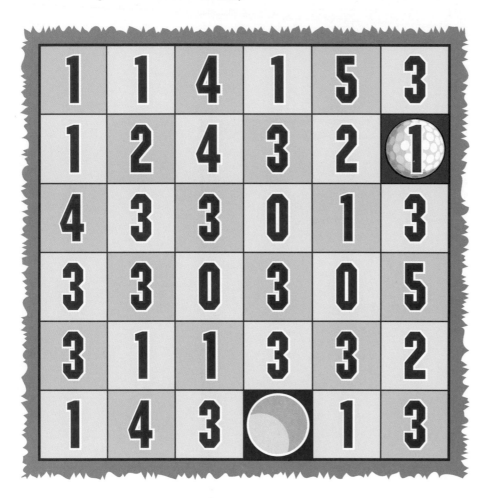

ONE LETTER LESS OR MORE

The word on the right side contains the letters of the word on the left side plus or minus the letter in the middle. One letter is already in the right place.

PAINTERS +R ☐ ☐ A ☐ ☐ ☐ ☐ ☐

★ Dynamic Duos by Peggy O'Shea

ACROSS
1 Rich soil
5 Urban's country cousin
10 Tropical food fish
14 French cheese
15 *Waterworld* girl
16 "Hey, sailor!"
17 "Surf City" duo
19 Queue
20 Artsy Manhattan area
21 Bent over
23 Sharp as a tack
26 Sicilian summer resort
27 *Civil Disobedience* essayist
29 Police snare
32 Domestic
33 Grand Central arrival
35 Tags on
36 Thurman in *Be Cool*
37 Beefeater, for one
38 Casino cube
39 Breads of India
41 Regaled
43 Diplomat's need
44 Ingratiates
46 Conclusions
48 Green gem
49 Fondue ingredient
50 Consecrated
53 Besides
54 Gas prefix
55 Rube Goldberg duo
60 Rowling's Beedle
61 Lend ___ (listen)
62 Seed case
63 Gross in *Coupe de Ville*
64 Nick in *Warrior*
65 Rip out

DOWN
1 JFK's successor
2 ___ pro nobis
3 Rhone tributary
4 Piano bar?
5 1988 James Belushi film
6 Rescind
7 Fish eggs
8 Sigh of sorrow
9 Jacklight
10 Lea who starred in *Miss Saigon*
11 Disney chipmunk duo
12 First-rate
13 Recolored
18 Middle C, e.g.
22 Three ___ match
23 Synchronize
24 Medicine man
25 Hanna-Barbera duo
28 Pushes
29 Inexpensive restaurant
30 Proclamations
31 Feared African fly
34 River islet
40 Coastal
41 Morgan who played God
42 "Well, I ___!"
43 "___ Afternoon": Moody Blues
45 Tennis scores
47 Avoid socially
50 Rum cake
51 *All in the Family* producer
52 *A Cat in Paris* cat
53 Bog moss
56 Mitchell in *Honeydripper*
57 Lyricist Gershwin
58 Reunion attendees
59 Bugling deer

★★ BrainSnack®—Skewered

Which kebab (1–6) does not belong?

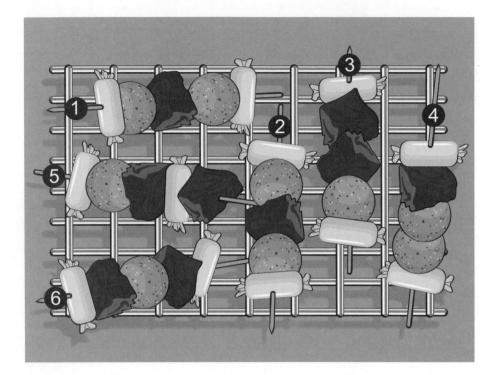

LETTER LINE

Put a letter in each of the squares below to make a word that is a conversion from one thing to another. The number clues refer to other words that can be made from the whole.

5 7 8 9 10 4 OVERSEE; 2 3 8 7 1 CHAOS;
1 2 6 8 10 7 4 V SIGN; 1 2 3 10 5 6 POWER UP;
2 3 4 5 9 10 FOR SUSPENDING

1	2	3	4	5	6	7	8	9	10

★ Word Sudoku

Complete the grid so that each row, each column and each 3 x 3 frame contains the nine letters from the black box below. The hidden nine-letter word is in the diagonal from top left to bottom right.

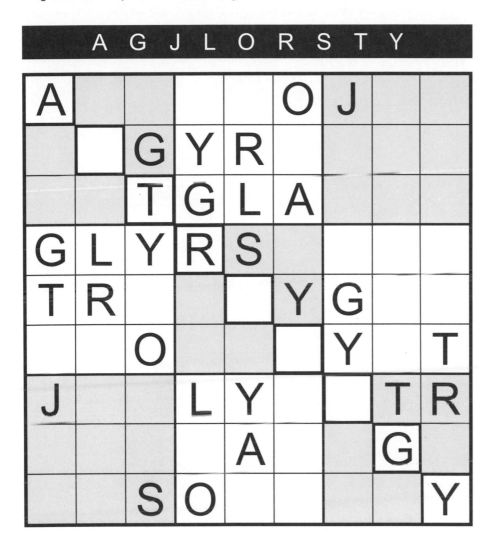

A G J L O R S T Y

UNCANNY TURN

Rearrange the letters of the phrase below to form a cognate anagram, one which is related or connected in meaning to the original phrase. The answer can be one or more words.

SWEN OR INGA

★ Loves by Cindy Wheeler

ACROSS

1 "Freeze!"
5 Campus near Beverly Hills
9 "The Rocket" of tennis
14 *Superman II* villainess
15 High time
16 Leave out, as a vowel
17 Edward Cullen's love
19 Self-evident fact
20 Zany trio
21 Ridiculous
23 Time of your life
24 Geometry calculation
25 Apparently pleased
29 Pierce in *GoldenEye*
32 Bakery goodie
33 Printed in an anthology
35 Charm with flowers and candy
36 Cream-filled snack
37 Court dance
38 Clothes
39 Olympic swimmer Thorpe
40 Greek Is
41 Bill of fare
42 Expurgate
44 Tabloid fodder
46 Feed the kitty
47 Cardiogram
48 Weasel relatives
51 Gets into something
55 Poet Ginsberg
56 Phantom of the Opera's love
58 Fishing rod attachments
59 "___ le Roi!" (Bastille cry)
60 *Night* author Wiesel
61 Concisely worded
62 Dashiki, e.g.
63 Angling gear

DOWN

1 Foot-long sandwiches
2 Waste allowance
3 Kon-Tiki Museum site
4 Silicon Valley city
5 Like Norm's wife on *Cheers*
6 Female whales
7 Hawaiian for "long"
8 Tolstoy heroine Karenina
9 Lower shackle
10 Flare-bottomed skirts
11 Edward's *Pretty Woman* love
12 Where Adam had a "deep sleep"
13 Glass designer Lalique
18 Texas A&M student
22 Clear wrap
25 Dispassionate
26 Upstanding
27 Sherlock's love
28 Prepare Parmesan
29 Chutzpah
30 Major artery
31 Dynamite inventor
34 Space walk, for short
37 Baffler
38 Hood
40 Deeply felt
41 Bakery buys
43 Heavenly beings
45 Vivid purplish red
48 Ms. Krabappel's nemesis
49 "Hard ___!" (ship command)
50 Wound mark
51 Not colorful
52 Granary
53 Arthurian lady
54 Bishoprics
57 Premium cable channel

★ Sudoku

Fill in the grid so that each row, each column and each 3 x 3 frame contains every number from 1 to 9.

		5						
			9	7		4		6
4	6			5		9		2
5	1						8	
					4	3		
7	2	4	3	8	6	5	9	1
		2		3			1	9
	5			2		8	6	

SYMBOL SUMS

Can you work out these number sums using three of these four symbols? **+ − ÷ ×**
(No fractions or minus numbers are involved in the sum as you progress from left to right.)

$$4 \square 3 \square 3 \square 3 = 3$$

★★ Sunny Weather

Where will the sun shine? With the knowledge that each arrow points to
a place where a symbol should be, can you locate the sunny spots? The
symbols cannot be next to each other vertically, horizontally or diagonally.
A symbol cannot be placed on top of an arrow. We show one symbol.

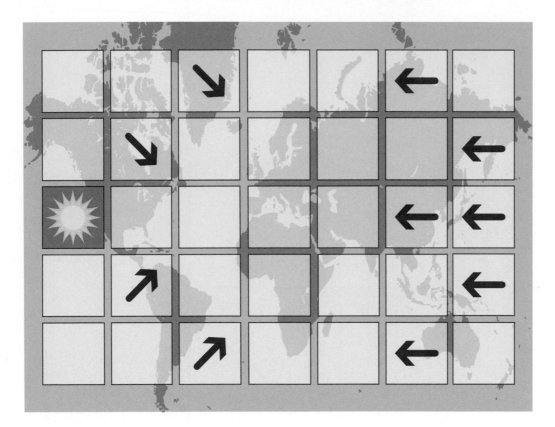

TRIANAGRAM

Three-word groups of anagrams are also called triplets or trianagrams.
Complete the group:

LIVERS   _ _ _ _ _ _   _ _ _ _ _ _

★ Flower Girls by Maggie Ellis

ACROSS

1 "___ Smile Be Your Umbrella"
5 Pontiff's garb
10 Disease suffix
14 *Diary of ___ Housewife* (1970)
15 Chinese green tea
16 Mile's equivalent?
17 Porky's love
19 "___ a Kick Out of You"
20 Eared marine animal
21 Venus and Serena, e.g.
23 Corrigenda
24 Like some misses
25 Orange beverage
27 Homesteader
30 Venerable English saint
33 Refines flour
35 One, in Oberhausen
36 Monroe in *Cold Mountain*
37 Angelina Jolie film
38 ROTC grads: Abbr.
39 Hawaiian neckwear
41 Heart line
43 Putin's refusal
44 Immediate
46 Carlisle Cullen's wife
48 Croquet spot
49 Place for a moat
53 Nook operating system
56 Relate
57 Make much of
58 *The Golden Girls* character
60 Of a kind
61 Made goo-goo eyes at
62 Foil relative
63 Angry
64 Saloon lights
65 "___ in the Clowns": Collins

DOWN

1 Concentration problem
2 Mideast VIP
3 One of Genghis Khan's horde
4 Admire a lot
5 Buckeyes
6 Gosling in *The Ides of March*
7 African cobra
8 Sci-fi author ___ McMaster Bujold
9 "Gentlemen, start your ___!"
10 Flatter, in a way
11 *Peter Pan* princess
12 Czech river
13 Mach 2 fliers, formerly
18 *The Concrete Jungle* actress Talbot
22 Stage scenery
26 1962 Jackie Gleason movie
27 License plate datum
28 Being, in Barcelona
29 Observe the Sabbath
30 *South Pacific* isle
31 First abode
32 Hazzard County girl
34 Christmas tree
40 Under way
41 Firewood support
42 Goes up
43 Cuddles
45 Orinoco tributary
47 Miss Poppins
50 Mole-colored
51 Some bedding
52 Was no more
53 *Volsunga Saga* king
54 Film ___ (movie genre)
55 Genoese magistrate
56 Hammer head
59 ___-Blo fuse

★ Futoshiki

Fill in the 5 x 5 grid with the numbers from 1 to 5 once per row and column, while following the greater than/lesser than symbols shown. There is only one valid solution that can be reached through logic and clear thinking alone!

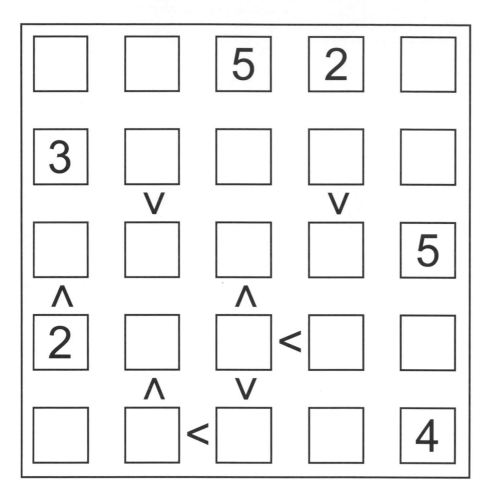

LETTERBLOCKS

Move the letterblocks around so that words are formed on top and below that you can associate with cameras. In some blocks, the letter from the top row has been switched with the letter from the bottom row.

★ BrainSnack®—Just Desserts

Which pudding container (1–6) has a printing error on the lid?

QUICK CROSSWORD

Place the countries listed below in the crossword grid.

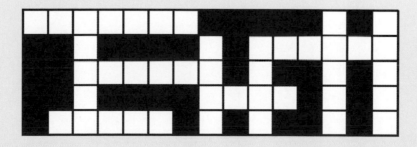

AUSTRIA RUSSIA GABON LAOS OMAN CHAD SAMOA SYRIA QATAR CANADA

★ Hobbies

All the words are hidden vertically, horizontally or diagonally—in both directions. The letters that remain unused form a sentence from left to right.

```
S H O B R A S S B A N D B B G
R S P H O T O G R A P H I E N
A T R A I N S P O T T I N G I
C B S E A R E A K P B U R M K
S A E R W U R I O H C R O O L
Y K R U E O T N O D Y R E D A
M E T T O A L T C H I U T E W
O B A A B T O F P G F I E L D
N R E R N T E A A N A R H T E
O E H E S T R M Y I R N C R E
R A T T C G I R O N T T O A L
T D A I I E S P E S D R I B
S C U L P T S P Q D E E C N M
A A L I T D L U W R H L O S A
D A R O K A I E M A C C T H G
C R P E N L Y A D G R Y R E D
O N A T T E F O R O O C P L E
K R O W H C T A P A M S U R E
```

DRAW
FLOWERS
GAMBLE
GARDENING
LITERATURE
MODEL
MODEL TRAINS
MUSIC
ORCHESTRA
ORIGAMI
PAINT
PATCHWORK
PHOTOGRAPH
PLANT
POTTERY
QUILT
SCULPT
THEATRE
TRAIN SPOTTING
WALKING

ASTRONOMY   BRASS BAND   CHOIR
BAKE BREAD   BREED   COOK
BATIK   CALLIGRAPHY   CROCHET
BIRDS   CARS   CYCLE

DELETE ONE

Delete one letter from PIONEER and find another first word.

★ 2012 Winners by Michele Sayer

ACROSS
1 Santa Fe's arty neighbor
5 Dame ___ Everage
9 Bluish gray
14 Summit
15 Clip-and-file item
16 Assign blame to
17 2012 Oscar winner for Best Film
19 Arboreal lemur
20 Motion detectors
21 Like the jack of hearts
23 Garden implement
24 Styptic pencil
25 Laughs for the knowing
29 Amount increases
32 Cocktail grouping
33 Wanderer
35 ___-A-Fella Records
36 Proboscis
37 Corsage spot
38 Guesstimate words
39 Suffix meaning "to the max"
40 Main artery
41 Cry from Ahab
42 Print anew
44 Night flights
46 Loch ___ Monster
47 Hide ___ hair
48 Shindigs
51 Pickles
55 Owlish utterances
56 2012 Grammy winner for "Otis"
58 Mini-map
59 Athena's breastplate
60 Stress-free living
61 Lecherous looks
62 "Jesus ___": John 11:35
63 Tried to fill an inside straight, e.g.

DOWN
1 Dice, slangily
2 Pain in the neck?
3 Prophetic sign
4 Where "she sells shells"
5 Chicken Kiev, e.g.
6 Podium
7 Constantine's birthplace
8 Choir voice
9 Pitched, in a sense
10 Starting ___
11 2012 Brisbane International winner
12 Moved quickly
13 Arthurian lady
18 Castles on a board
22 Brazilian seaport
25 2012 winner over Djokovic at Indian Wells
26 Calf grabber
27 2012 WGC-Cadillac Championship winner
28 Pitfall
29 Eyeliner problem
30 Deputized group
31 Glaswegians
34 Choose "yes," e.g.
37 Despicable person
38 Blown away
40 Hockey stats
41 Truly love
43 Volleyball position
45 Form into a sac
48 TV doctor
49 Top-rated
50 Turn aside
51 Salon sound
52 Prickly ___ (cactus)
53 Existence, to Caesar
54 Ragout
57 We do it every second

★ Spot the Differences

Find the nine differences in the image on the right.

DOUBLETALK

Homophones are words that share the same pronunciation, no matter how they are spelled. If they are spelled differently then they are called heterographs. Find heterographs meaning:

ACCLAIM and PETITIONS DEVOUTLY

★ Sudoku X

Fill in the grid so that each row, each column and each 3 x 3 frame contains every number from 1 to 9. The two main diagonals of the grid also contain every number from 1 to 9.

		6						
						5	1	
				2	7	8	3	
			2					
		4		6	5	9		3
9				8		2		
7				9				
	4					6	5	8
2	6	8	5	4			7	9

BLOCK ANAGRAM

Form the words that are described in the brackets with the letters above the grid. Extra letters are already in the right place.

MOONSTAR *(stargazer)*

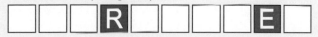

★ Alphabet Trios by Tim Wagner

ACROSS

1 ___ breve (2/2 time)
5 Blazer
9 AOL access
14 Vientiane locale
15 Heraldic wreath
16 Sports venue
17 Principals' degrees
18 Elite Eight org.
19 White-water craft
20 Franco-American incident of 1797–98
22 Coastal recess
23 Swiss canton
24 *Picnic* playright
25 Mother-of-pearl source
29 Church tower
32 Liability
33 Cereal fungus
35 Rest-and-restoration spots
36 Bowlike line
37 Wheaton in *Stand by Me*
38 Work in a studio
39 Part of YMCA
41 Fragrant blossom
43 Manitoba tribe
44 Cowboy hat
46 "___ Perfect": Miley Cyrus
48 Stumble
49 Tattoo word
50 Martin's *Laugh-In* partner
52 Amsterdam airport booking
58 "___ came a spider..."
59 ___ contendere
60 Shell team
61 Amalgamate
62 Mideast prince
63 Gas prefix
64 "For goodness ___!"
65 Twiddle one's thumbs
66 City of SE France

DOWN

1 O'Loughlin of *Hawaii Five-O*
2 "___ Madonna": Beatles
3 City in Poland
4 1946 Triple Crown winner
5 Intern
6 Two-colored whale
7 Basque word for "merry"
8 Whiz
9 "Semper Fi" soldier
10 Florida fruits
11 "Let's Get Rocked" group
12 Dresden duck
13 Tall spar
21 To and ___

24 *Addams Family* cousin
25 Maud in *Octopussy*
26 French hat
27 *The View* airer
28 Stu in *The Bride Came C.O.D.*
29 Blue-billed bird
30 Tyne Daly role
31 Will in *Blue Bloods*
34 Grissom of *CSI*
40 Outlandish
41 Prune
42 Solace
43 Rib-tickling
45 Burns the tips
47 Former NBAer Manute
50 Butts into
51 Olive genus
52 "If You ___ Susie"
53 Arizona hill

54 Cato's 1052
55 *Agnes* ___: Brontë
56 Medal recipient, say
57 Artemis, to Apollo

★ BrainSnack®—Numbers Game

Which number (1–7) appears most frequently?

1 4 1 5 3
1 3 6 6 6 4 1
2 2 2 7 6
7 2 4
4 7
5 6 7 4 6
4

QUICK WORD SEARCH

Find the words listed below in the word search grid.

B	T	R	E	E	C	H	A	I	R	T	C	V	T	Y
I	P	A	T	I	O	V	E	R	A	N	D	A	H	P
R	C	D	W	Y	H	O	R	I	Z	O	N	S	Y	A
D	G	A	K	C	L	O	U	D	S	J	V	M	N	T
S	F	S	Z	H	A	F	L	O	W	E	R	S	C	H

TREE PATH SKY CLOUDS PATIO FLOWERS VERANDAH CHAIR BIRDS HORIZON

★ Kakuro

Each number in a black area is the sum of the numbers that you have to enter in the next empty boxes. The empty boxes that make up the sum are called a run. The sum of the across run is written above the diagonal in the black area and the sum of the down run is written below the diagonal. Runs can only contain the numbers 1 through 9 and each number in a run can only be used once. The gray boxes only contain odd numbers and the white only even numbers.

DOUBLETALK

Homophones are words that share the same pronunciation, no matter how they are spelled. If they are spelled differently then they are called heterographs. Find heterographs meaning:

WAGER and A SLICE OF MEAT

★ Answer Grid by Don Law

ACROSS
1 Frontman's backup
5 Ring ___ (sound familiar)
10 Prolific author?
14 Wind-ensemble instrument
15 Wayward calf
16 Lose heart
17 1982 Luciano Pavarotti film
19 "Alice's Restaurant" officer
20 ___ of the Sorrows: Synge
21 Hurt
23 Virus variety
24 Scottish island
25 Fathomless
27 "___ at All": Beatles
30 Auntie of Broadway
33 Beatrice's adorer
35 NY Giants guard Chris
36 Chicken ___ king
37 Mount a diamond
38 Corn spike
39 Country singer Collin
41 Unemotional
43 Flat plinth, in architecture
44 Quiver or tremble
46 Former KISS drummer Eric
48 Dubai VIP
49 Thread's partner
53 Environment
56 Word jumble
57 Susan in Beauty and the Beast
58 Shilly-shallier's answer
60 Kathryn of Law & Order: CI
61 Down the hatch
62 "... and ___ the twain shall meet"
63 Deposits, as eggs
64 Takes a card from the deck
65 Suburb of Paris

DOWN
1 Enesco plush bears
2 Red as___
3 Private answer?
4 Lower in stature
5 Trimmed
6 One who makes you yawn
7 Tempera ingredient
8 Year Trajan was born
9 Like Aslan
10 Check boxes
11 Super-easy decision
12 Role for Ronny Howard
13 State of misfortune
18 "Thus with a kiss ___": Shak.
22 Delight
26 Collage adhesive
27 Dusty storage room
28 "You Can Call ___": Simon
29 Younger Saarinen
30 Former Met Throneberry
31 Kyrgyzstan mountains
32 1958 Buddy Holly song
34 Classical intro?
40 White weasels
41 Wandered off
42 Mortars
43 Pizza spice
45 British isle
47 Clean a pipe
50 Household appliance
51 Put a tag on
52 It may be at your fingertips
53 Cad
54 Taj Mahal city
55 Wardrobe malfunction
56 From the top
59 MARTA stop: Abbr.

★ Sudoku Twin

Fill in the grid so that each row, each column and each 3 x 3 frame contains every number from 1 to 9. A sudoku twin is two connected 9 x 9 sudokus.

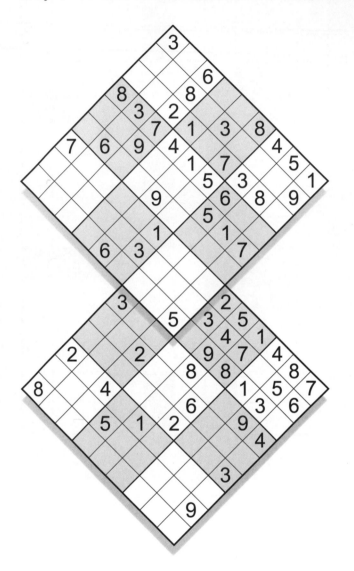

TRIANAGRAM

Three-word groups of anagrams are also called triplets or trianagrams.
Complete the group:

A S L E E P   _ _ _ _ _ _   _ _ _ _ _ _

★★ Keep Going

Start on a blank square of your choice and connect as many blank squares as possible with one single continuous line. You can only connect squares along vertical and horizontal lines. You must continue the connecting line up until the next obstacle, i.e., the rim of the box, a black square or a square that has already been used. You can change direction at any obstacle you meet. Each square can be used only once. The number of blank squares that will be left unused is marked in the upper square. There is more than one solution. We show only one solution.

FRIENDS?

What do the following words have in common?

ACHIEVE CLASS CHARGE CARRIAGE FOOT

★ Black and White by Brian O'Shea

ACROSS

1 Handball need
5 Uncontrollable twitch
10 Oates of hockey
14 Marine heading
15 Word on a name tag
16 Olin of *Hollywood Homicide*
17 Butter bean
18 "___ your instructions ..."
19 Former Gabon president Bongo
20 Black-and-white animal
22 2011 black-and-white film
24 Idolized ones
26 Omega preceder
27 Of birth
30 Symbol of justice
35 Costa del ___
38 *The Time Machine* race
40 Roman title
41 Black-and-white verbal challenge
45 Chipmunk snack
46 Organic compound
47 Interrogate
48 Fair maiden
50 In the air
53 Dignitary
55 Architect's offering
59 Black-and-white dog
65 Black-and-white equine
66 Frankenstein's helper
67 Downs in Surrey
69 Romanov ruler
70 Cocky
71 Nostalgic style
72 Sam Cooke's "You ___ Me"
73 Take to heart
74 Snail-mail item
75 Opposite of exo-

DOWN

1 *America's Most Wanted* host
2 Resembling
3 Large-eyed primate
4 Pressure
5 Doo-wop group ___ Na Na
6 Gnat or brat
7 *Kubla Khan* river
8 Shuteye
9 Entangling quagmire
10 Considerably
11 Moore in *Disclosure*
12 Duck genus
13 Merchandise center
21 New Zealand parrot
23 Houston campus, for short
25 Mulligan ___
28 Lotion additive

29 Luft or Doone
31 Wood dresser
32 Minnelli in *Cabaret*
33 Building annexes
34 Hunt up
35 Pompano relative
36 Large dolphin
37 Come into view
39 False deity
42 SAT takers: Abbr.
43 1983 Indy 500 winner Tom
44 Muddle along
49 Metric measurements
51 Shriner's hat
52 Dangerous African fly
54 Laboratory tube
56 Norwegian playwright
57 Thousand
58 Henner on *Taxi*
59 Kind of antenna

60 Malarial condition
61 Source of tradition
62 TV palomino
63 Nora Charles' dog
64 Average
68 Shaggy locks

★★★ Sport Maze

Draw the shortest way from the ball to the goal. You can only move along vertical and horizontal lines, not along diagonal lines. The figure on each square indicates the number of squares the ball must be moved in the same direction. You can change direction at each stop.

3	1	2	4	5	4
3	3	2	1	3	2
4	1	1	0	○	0
3	2	2	1	2	3
4	3	3	2	4	5
2	2	1	4	1	1

ONE LETTER LESS OR MORE

The word on the right side contains the letters of the word on the left side plus or minus the letter in the middle. One letter is already in the right place.

E I N S T E I N -I ☐ ☐ T ☐ ☐ ☐ ☐

★ BrainSnack®—True Romance

Who (Elsie, Mary, Annie or Carey) is Ryan's girlfriend?

DOODLE PUZZLE

A doodle puzzle is a combination of images, letters and/or numbers that represent a word or a concept. If you cannot solve a doodle puzzle, do not look at the answer right away. Think hard—and outside the box.

★ Reds by Peggy O'Shea

ACROSS

1 Polynesian pantomine dance
5 Fashion fold
10 Raleigh locale: Abbr.
14 *The Plague* setting
15 Witherspoon in *This Means War*
16 French department
17 *No, No, Nanette* actress
19 Don Corleone
20 Boar's weapon
21 Twin sister of Apollo
23 Set a high goal
26 Is bedbound
27 Attire
29 Spa headrests
32 Cannes film
33 Goshawk claw
35 Work without ___ (be daring)
36 Variety
37 Suffix with neat or beat
38 Seafarer
39 "Fat chance!"
41 Sum finder
43 Lake fish
44 It'll bring you down
46 Two make a score
48 Hornet's home
49 *Coal ___ Daughter* (1980)
50 Strategic withdrawal
53 Marquand detective
54 Ibuprofen target
55 Select the best and leave the rest
60 ___ *All That* (1999)
61 Great Lakes memory aid
62 Petty in *Free Willy*
63 Anchorage
64 Succumb to time and tide
65 "How Deep is ___ Love": Bee Gees

DOWN

1 Old Testament mount
2 Mufasa's mother
3 Yellow dog
4 Available 24/7
5 Party favor
6 Soup veggie
7 Unagi at the sushi bar
8 Like the Owl and the Pussycat
9 Lay of the land
10 *Animal Farm* is one
11 2011 NCAA football champs
12 Not for
13 Antique autos
18 Honshu seaport
22 "___ I Kissed You": Everly Brothers
23 Curving
24 Sinbad, for one
25 Cartoon cat
28 Jessica in *Cocoon*
29 Jabbed in the ribs
30 More watered down
31 Fast-lane woe
34 Jack-in-the-box part
40 Site of a 1953 conquest
41 Case for an attorney?
42 Deep regret
43 Splendid array
45 Suffix for expert
47 Vatican ___
50 Rough talk
51 Sympathetic response
52 2011 superhero film
53 Wilbur Post's horse
56 Unrestrained musical genre
57 Perfect grade
58 French vineyard
59 Cassis aperitif

★ Tea

All the words are hidden vertically, horizontally or diagonally—in both directions. The letters that remain unused form a sentence from left to right.

```
M W H E N T H E S T E E P L E
A S N G E L E A R L G R E Y I
S O S B D H H A B N G A V C E
S B A L I F T B O E V E H L R
A I C A S N U L R E W A A I O
R O O C N B O A S A M P L P R
E O O K I O U B T O S I M T U
D R K S A O L E M A Q O I O K
W B I T T E R I N U O N N N O
O A G T N R L G O W H I T E Y
P T R D U E A R A N I H C H G
N E E M O A I I N O L Y E C A
U T E H M C L E N Y D R R I N
G E N I E F F A C E B K V E R
S O F T W O O D Y S R S T R O
N G E T N I M R E P P E P T E
R A V O M A S A W I T H L O T
S O F M I L K A N D S U G A R
```

GUNPOWDER
GYOKURO
HERBS
ICE TEA
LAPSANG
LEAVES
LIPTON
LIQUORICE
MINT
MOUNTAINSIDE
OOLONG
PEPPERMINT
RITUAL
ROOIBOS
SAMOVAR
SOFTWOOD
STEEP
STRAINER
TOUAREG
WARM
WATER
WHITE

ASSAM
BITTER
BLACK
BLEND
BUBBLE
CAFFEINE
CEYLON
CHAMOMILE
CHINA
COOK
EARL GREY
GREEN

DELETE ONE

Delete one letter from GREAT ON VISITS and find one who is.

★ Word Sudoku

Complete the grid so that each row, each column and each 3 x 3 frame contains the nine letters from the black box below. The hidden nine-letter word is in the diagonal from top left to bottom right.

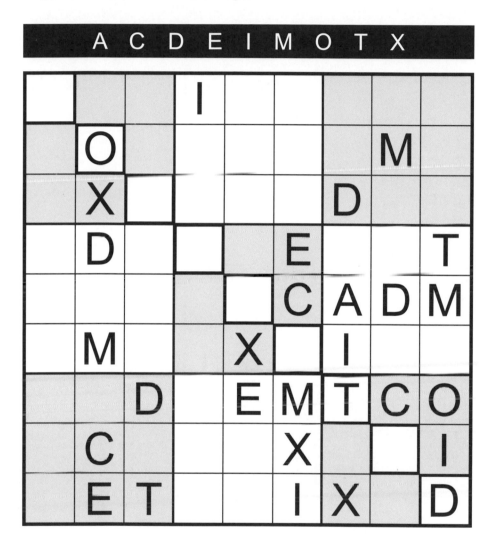

A	C	D	E	I	M	O	T	X

UNCANNY TURN

Rearrange the letters of the phrase below to form a cognate anagram, one which is related or connected in meaning to the original phrase. The answer can be one or more words.

A CENT TIP

★ Binairo

Complete the grid with zeros and ones until there are 6 zeros and 6 ones in every row and every column. No more than two of the same number can be next to or under each other. Rows or columns with exactly the same content are not allowed. There is only one valid solution.

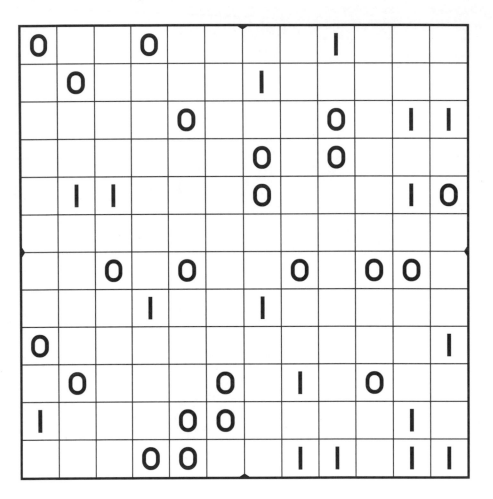

SYMBOL SUMS

Can you work out these number sums using three of these four symbols? **+ − ÷ ×**
(No fractions or minus numbers are involved in the sum as you progress from left to right.)

$$9 \;\square\; 3 \;\square\; 5 \;\square\; 6 = 48$$

★★ '60s Hits by John M. Samson

ACROSS

1 Race length
5 Hurdles for doctors-to-be
10 Soldering tool
14 Ireland, in poetry
15 *Air Music* composer
16 *Peter Pan* dog
17 "Soul Man" duo
19 Does Easter eggs
20 Their motto is "Can Do!"
21 Unlawful
23 Celtic god of the sea
24 Jacob's first wife
25 Revised
29 Like a junior miss
32 Audible dashes
33 Executed a gainer
35 Like much of Saudi Arabia
36 Suffix for Capri
37 ___ *for Corpse*: Grafton
38 *Love Story* composer
39 "Queen of Country" McEntire
41 Fender-bender results
43 Teller's partner
44 Built
46 Maine capital
48 At the vertex
49 Guy's mate
50 Dovish
53 Term of endearment
57 Thin necktie
58 "Oh, Pretty Woman" singer
60 Kid Rock hit
61 Kind of union
62 St. Petersburg river
63 1979 Polanski film
64 Church council
65 Stretch out

DOWN

1 Army chow
2 "Dies ___" (Requiem Mass hymn)
3 Peru capital
4 Allows
5 Called for a pizza
6 Curtain hardware
7 Lofty altar
8 Eshkol of Israel
9 Seemed funny
10 Hoosier State
11 "Hit the Road Jack" singer
12 R.E.M.'s "The ___ Love"
13 GOP Elephant creator
18 When pigs fly, to poets
22 Marvin in *Cat Ballou*
25 Flip over
26 Some time after
27 "She Loves You" group
28 Cubed
29 Kernel's coat
30 "Jack and the Beanstalk" heavy
31 Jennifer's *Ab Fab* role
34 Car ID
40 They speak louder than words
41 Exits the premises
42 Sweetened
43 Taffy making step
45 Ski lift
47 Distinctive clothing
50 Blind as ___
51 Iditarod Trail's end
52 Irish golfer McIlroy
53 Extinct bird
54 Czech river
55 De ___ (from square one)
56 Chew like a beaver
59 PBS chef of *Can Cook* fame

★ Horoscope

Fill in the grid so that every row, every column and every frame of six boxes contains six different symbols: health, work, money, happiness, family and love. Look at the row or column that corresponds with your sign of the zodiac and find out which of the six symbols are important for you today. The symbols appear in increasing order of importance (1–6). It's up to you to translate the meaning of each symbol to your specific situation.

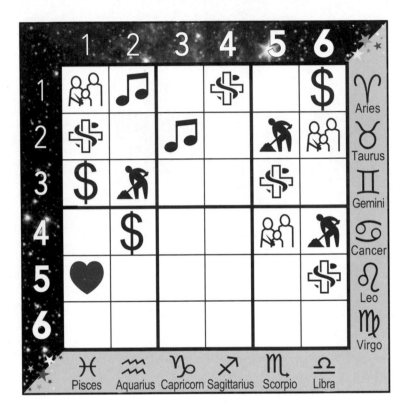

WORD WALL

Beginning at the left side of the wall, make a word by adding one group of letters from each column as you move left to right. When you have found the first word, go back to the second column and start the next word, gathering one group of letters from each column, and so on until all the letters are used to make six words.

★★ BrainSnack®—Shaping

Which shape (1–6) contains more white than black?

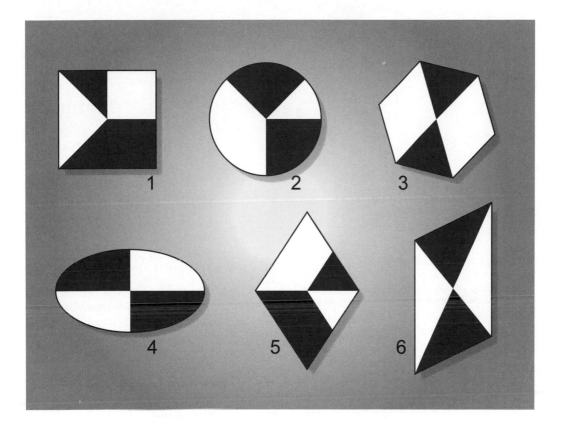

TRIANAGRAM

Three-word groups of anagrams are also called triplets or trianagrams.
Complete the group:

BAKER _ _ _ _ _   _ _ _ _ _

★★ '70s Hits by John M. Samson

ACROSS

1 Oleo squares
5 Darfur's land
10 In the clear for a pass
14 Large land mass
15 Trailer, for one
16 Take the bus
17 "Stayin' Alive" group
19 *Picnic* playwright
20 Apartment balcony
21 Pulled an oar
23 Declare firmly
24 Liesl von Trapp's love
25 ___-do-well
27 Curiosity piece
30 Copier brand
33 *Boléro* composer
35 40-decibel unit
36 Suffix for sheep
37 ___ Aviv
38 Supporter's vote
39 Middle marks
41 ___ four (teacake)
43 Sandler in *Jack and Jill*
44 Zoo bosses
46 Disraeli's nobility
48 Verdi heroine
49 Melancholy
53 Member of the lumpenproletariat
56 Tearoom urn
57 "___ Want to Do": Sugarland
58 "So Far Away" singer
60 "___ Around": Beach Boys
61 Act theatrically
62 Prefix for skeleton
63 Laddie's love
64 Floor samples
65 Breather

DOWN

1 "Too Many Tears" singer LaBelle
2 Grayish
3 Cake layers
4 Audrey Hepburn film
5 Ghost
6 Egg on
7 Nanny goat
8 City near Des Moines
9 Nasal opening
10 1970 World Series winners
11 "Another Brick in the Wall" group
12 Ford SUV
13 "When I ___ You": Sayer
18 Take the pressure off
22 Good name for a thief

26 Scores
27 Contradict
28 ___-Day vitamins
29 Play mates?
30 Rocker Jagger
31 "Of course!"
32 "Hotel California" group
34 Track doc
40 Hard stuff
41 Strutted about
42 Enchilada cousins
43 *Today* weatherman
45 Child-care author LeShan
47 "Tosca" setting
50 Kind of like ewe
51 White ___ Missile Range
52 Grain fungus

53 Colorado ski resort
54 Sea lettuce
55 Change from wild to mild
56 ___ speak (as it were)
59 Gypsy boy

★ Sudoku

Fill in the grid so that each row, each column and each 3 x 3 frame contains every number from 1 to 9.

4	1	5			3			7
	8	2	5	4	7		6	
6	3		9	1		8		5
	7	4		6		5		
2				5		1		9
				2		6		4
1					5			
		8				2		

SYMBOL SUMS

Can you work out these number sums using three of these four symbols? **+ − ÷ ×**
(No fractions or minus numbers are involved in the sum as you progress from left to right.)

$$8 \ \square \ 3 \ \square \ 9 \ \square \ 3 = 11$$

★★ Number Cluster

Complete the grid by constituting adjoining clusters that consist of as many cubes as the number on the cubes. At cube 5, for instance, you will have to make a five-cube cluster. Two or more figure cubes of the same value belong to the same cluster. You can only place your cubes along horizontal and/or vertical lines.

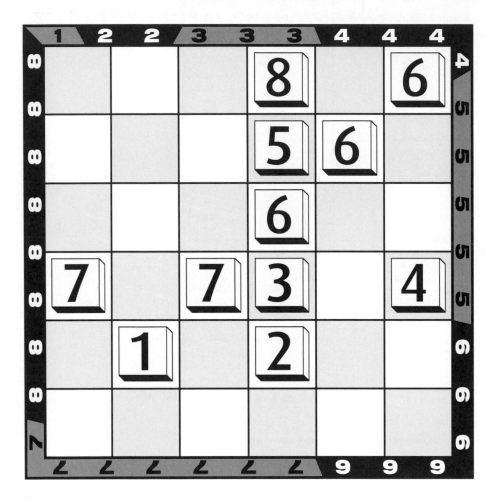

SANDWICH

What five-letter word belongs between the word on the left and the word on the right, so that the first and second word, and the second and third word, each form a common compound word or phrase?

WING _ _ _ _ _ PERSON

★★ '80s Hits by John M. Samson

ACROSS

1 Husband of Sita
5 Courtroom rituals
10 Purim month
14 Enthusiastic liveliness
15 Brown ermine
16 Guy
17 "Let's Dance" singer
19 Faucet defect
20 Sitting
21 Says again and again
23 Rocky outcrop
24 Sean in *The Tree of Life*
25 "Like a Virgin" singer
29 *Arabian Nights* hero
32 Egyptian sun god
33 Lose topsoil
35 Angelic glow
36 Two-minute warning giver
37 E-address
38 "Radio Song" group
39 Dry sprinkle
41 Gradually declined
43 *West of the Pecos* author Grey
44 "You Can Do Magic" group
46 Had longings
48 Advil unit
49 Joke
50 Nemo or Bligh
53 Grand Canyon State
57 Jai tail
58 "We Belong" singer
60 One in on a bust
61 Shoulder warmer
62 Tisha's *Martin* role
63 Word with split and rear
64 Basso Simon ___
65 Picket line crosser

DOWN

1 1981 Warren Beatty film
2 Amor's wings
3 Dallas cagers
4 Jennifer in *Just Go With It*
5 "One of Us" singer Joan
6 "This must weigh ___!"
7 Wrecker at wrecks
8 Flynn's ladder in *Tangled*
9 Place for a bell
10 Appendices
11 "A View to a Kill" group
12 Miner's ingress
13 Sales staff members
18 Singer Celine
22 Kind of shooter
25 Atlanta transit system
26 Special Forces force
27 "Love Bites" group
28 Resort off Venezuela
29 Grace of *Will & Grace*
30 Rich or Worth
31 Dubbed
34 Sun or planet
40 Judges
41 2010 Taylor Lautner film
42 Six ___ of separation
43 Weaves back and forth
45 Dockworkers union: Abbr.
47 ___ in the neck
50 Raspberry stem
51 The ___ Parsons Project
52 DC ball club
53 Sufficiently talented
54 Psych suffix
55 Wendy's St. Bernard
56 Libyan or Lebanese
59 Shaver

★★ Concentration—Place 100

Mentally calculate under what letter the number 100 should appear.

a	b	c	d	e	f	g	h
1	2	3	4	5	6	7	8
9	10	11	12	13	14	15	16
17	18	19	20	.	.	.	.
.	.	.	.	.	.	.	.

LETTER LINE

Put a letter in each of the squares below to make a word which will brighten things up.
The number clues refer to other words which can be made from the whole.

5 4 4 10 7 2 9 ADULT MALE CHICKEN;
3 4 6 10 7 2 5 DRINK MAT; 5 2 6 3 7 4 9 10
CONTROLLING STRUCTURES; 3 5 2 6 7 8 9 ORIGINATOR;
3 2 1 6 5 CONIFER

1	2	3	4	5	6	7	8	9	10

★ BrainSnack®—Runaway Train

Which shadow (1–5) is the correct shadow of the toy train?

CHANGELINGS

Each of the three lines of letters below spell words which describe qualities useful for students, but the letters have been mixed up. Four letters from the first word are now in the third line, four letters from the third word are in the second line and four letters from the second word are in the first line. The remaining letters are in their original places. What are the words?

C D E A E T N E S N
N E D I C F D I O C
C O L V I R E N S E

★★ '90s Hits by John M. Samson

ACROSS
1 Weepy, tearful gasps
5 Teacher's charge
10 Area 51 phenomena
14 Front end
15 "Stormy Weather" singer
16 Early bedtime hour
17 "Where Does My Heart Beat Now" singer
19 Italia capital
20 Apple-pie order
21 British noble
23 Cool, to a retro hipster
24 Honduran seaport
25 Weapons pile
29 *Babes in ___* (1934)
32 He had a lion's lines
33 Send to a specialist
35 Box for fun
36 Dutch piano center
37 Ballpark drink
38 Air pressure abbr.
39 Jaguars and Cougars
41 Old French coin
43 Bacon measure
44 Neon cousin
46 Clemens and L. Jackson
48 Edward of limerick fame
49 Libertarian Paul
50 Gaming areas
53 Computer memory
57 Chocolate type
58 "Wannabe" singers
60 Island group off New Guinea
61 Basin or bore preceder
62 Catch unawares
63 Bryn ___ College
64 Gets top billing
65 Spanish compass direction

DOWN
1 Pet-loving org.
2 Baseball pitcher Hershiser
3 Whirled weapon
4 Michael Phelps, notably
5 Monterey Jack, for one
6 Miner's bonanza
7 *Entourage* character Gold
8 One looking down on the "little people"
9 Ottawa hockey player
10 Spreads out, as a sleeping bag
11 "Criminal" singer
12 "Drinks are ___!"
13 Do ushering
18 Bright time
22 Coronación VIP
25 Smart-___ (wise guy)
26 Meteorological tool
27 "All I Wanna Do" singer
28 Pay attention in class
29 Preadults
30 Sounding congested
31 Small amounts
34 Sunshine State: Abbr.
40 One at the podium
41 Logging areas
42 Drug enterprises
43 It may brighten your morning
45 Dollop
47 *Switched-On Bach* synthesizer
50 Dr. Bricker on *The Love Boat*
51 ___ avis (one of a kind)
52 Use a cuspidor
53 Damage permanently
54 Wiles
55 Surfeit
56 Feudal thrall
59 Eddie Cantor's wife

★ Fast Food

All the words are hidden vertically, horizontally or diagonally—in both directions. The letters that remain unused form a sentence from left to right.

```
T H E D A N O M E L E S A S L
O W O F O O E S T U N Z K H D
M O O V B A B E K E Z C M A E
F N T I T X I M L I A R T W Y
S P O B P P O S P N E V O A R
E D A T O A F A S G V S T R T
F L O E O L D A R Y I N Y M S
L D F W H O A U L T T N H A U
T S T R O C B K E I A P T R D
S E E S E M E E F S R S L S N
O C R V A N E T A E C R A E I
T U T H R A C C L B U E E L D
I A G Y R O S H A O L G H G E
R S U G A R I U F T G A N N X
O P I O N A L P A R N N U I T
D I D R H O T D O G I E E R R
G D I O N A L L E Z T E R P A
C Y T T A F L U I S I T S N E
```

FRENCH FRIES
GYROS
HAMBURGER
HOT DOG
INDUSTRY
KEBAB
KETCHUP
LEMONADE
LUCRATIVE
MEATBALL
NUTS
OBESITY
OVEN
PIZZA
PRETZEL
PRINGLES
SHAWARMA
SNACKS
SUGAR
TEENAGERS
TRAIL MIX
UNHEALTHY

CHEAP
COLA
DIP SAUCE
DORITOS
EGG ROLL
EXTRA
FALAFEL
FATTY
FOOD

DELETE ONE

Delete one letter from AIM BALLS FOR THIS EDGE and find the game.

★★ Sunny Weather

Where will the sun shine? With the knowledge that each arrow points to a place where a symbol should be, can you locate the sunny spots? The symbols cannot be next to each other vertically, horizontally or diagonally. A symbol cannot be placed on top of an arrow. We show one symbol.

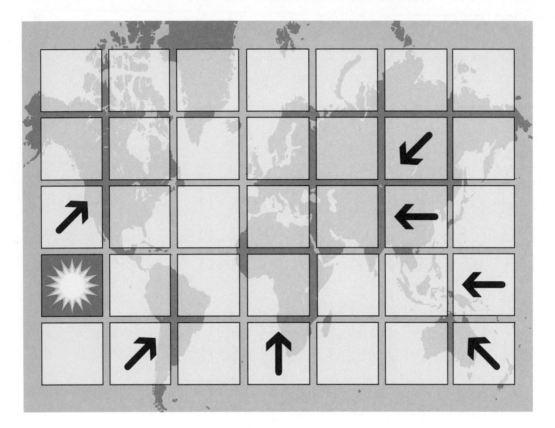

TRIANAGRAM

Three-word groups of anagrams are also called triplets or trianagrams.
Complete the group:

DUSTER   _ _ _ _ _ _   _ _ _ _ _ _

★★ '00s Hits by John M. Samson

ACROSS

1 Land in a depression
5 Jeweler's glass
10 Joyous
14 Waxed cheese
15 DuPont acrylic fiber
16 Lacoste founder Lacoste
17 "You're Beautiful" singer
19 Geraldine Chaplin's mom
20 *The Devil's Dictionary* author Bierce
21 Killed by submergence
23 Make believe
24 Italian summer resort
25 Crept up on
29 Sports page listings
32 Stick fast
33 Brother of Romulus
35 Father of François
36 Black cuckoo
37 Slow pitch
38 Wheaton of *Star Trek: TNG*
39 Bridal shower
41 Botanical shelter
43 Seven Dwarfs' workplace
44 Christmas tree trimming
46 Formidable foe
48 *GoldenEye* villain Trevelyan
49 Have some catching up to do
50 Some native Canadians
53 Do the voice-over
57 Two-___ (ballroom dance)
58 "Party in the U.S.A." singer
60 Hula hoops and yo-yos
61 Parisian school
62 Displays
63 Building projection
64 Bard of old
65 Geese that rarely swim

DOWN

1 "___ Vu": Warwick
2 Rock star Ant
3 Moussaka meat
4 Gemstone
5 Maine delicacy
6 Heraldic border
7 Curved Eskimo knife
8 Pollywog's home
9 Plats du jour
10 Like Peter Pan in *Hook*
11 "Bleeding Love" singer
12 Bancroft or Murray
13 The Grateful ___
18 Anklet
22 Put-___ (spoofs)
25 Lamb Chop's friend Lewis
26 Mixologist's mixer
27 "No One" singer
28 Site of an oracle of Apollo
29 Blades in *Predator 2*
30 "If I Had a Hammer" singer Lopez
31 Monica of tennis
34 Trim a fairway
40 High-level cover-up?
41 Turns into
42 Passed the baton
43 *Sleepless in Seattle* star
45 Moon craft, for short
47 Mr. Chagall
50 "Cómo ___ usted?"
51 Street sign
52 Ailing
53 Paramour of England's Charles II
54 Indy-winner Luyendyk
55 Move
56 Latin 101 infinitive
59 Mauna ___

★★ Keep Going

Start on a blank square of your choice and connect as many blank squares as possible with one single continuous line. You can only connect squares along vertical and horizontal lines. You must continue the connecting line up until the next obstacle, i.e., the rim of the box, a black square or a square that has already been used. You can change direction at any obstacle you meet. Each square can be used only once. The number of blank squares that will be left unused is marked in the upper square. There is more than one solution. We show only one solution.

FRIENDS?

What do the following words have in common?

BERRY BOTTLE GRASS BLOOD PRINT FISH

★★★ Sport Maze

Draw the shortest way from the ball to the goal. You can only move along vertical and horizontal lines, not along diagonal lines. The figure on each square indicates the number of squares the ball must be moved in the same direction. You can change direction at each stop.

5	●	4	3	3	5
4	3	1	4	4	1
1	1	1	1	3	1
4	1	1	3	2	1
4	0	4	3	4	2
5	2	2	5	4	5

ONE LETTER LESS OR MORE

The word on the right side contains the letters of the word on the left side plus or minus the letter in the middle. One letter is already in the right place.

F A R E W E L L ⊥ ☐ ☐ ☐ F ☐ ☐ ☐

★★ Sticks and Stones by Mary Leonard

ACROSS
1 Three Stooges blow
5 Squash rebound
10 Electric GM car
14 Trevi Fountain request
15 With mouth wide open
16 Dunkable cookie
17 "An apple ___ keeps ..."
18 Schnozz-related
19 Praise for toreadors
20 STICKS
23 *ER* setting
24 Ark unit
25 Drop
29 Pressurized spray
33 Cantina pot
34 Capital near the Gulf of Tonkin
36 *The Aviator* airline
37 STONES
41 Probable lifetime
42 Santa Clara chip maker
43 Laine of jazz
44 Absolute rulers
46 Rolle and Williams
49 Irish sea god
50 Lao-tzu's principle
51 "Sticks and stones ___ ..."
60 Tricky move
61 Group of TV experts
62 Franco in *Camelot*
63 River of Hesse
64 Peace goddess
65 Good's counterpart
66 Grunge
67 "Monopoly" cards
68 Leaf collector

DOWN
1 Quid pro quo
2 Italian resort island
3 Quickly, in memos
4 Bodily
5 Mexican island resort
6 "I've got ___ she's Big Foot Sal ..."
7 Level to the ground, in London
8 Colorful fish
9 Small reed organ
10 Witchcraft
11 Architectural fillet
12 Salacious glance
13 Pitch
21 Cold cube
22 Gruesome
25 Robert of *The 39 Steps*
26 Thomas Gray work
27 More foxy
28 "___ all, folks!"
29 Lizard
30 Snatched
31 Team bigwig
32 Populous African city
35 1952 hit "Botch-___"
38 Eatery in *The Sting*
39 Sporty Dodge
40 Grand Banks vessel
45 Alligator in *Pogo*
47 Does a salon job
48 Keyboard key
51 "A horse is a horse" horse
52 Bavarian car company
53 River to the North Sea
54 River rising in the Bernese Alps
55 Shinbone end
56 Darn with thread
57 Gulf of Finland feeder
58 Composer Satie
59 A flatfish

★ BrainSnack®—Axe Man

Which guitar (1–6) does not belong?

DOUBLETALK

Homophones are words that share the same pronunciation, no matter how they are spelled.
If they are spelled differently then they are called heterographs. Find heterographs meaning:

WRITING MATERIALS and NOT MOVING

★ Word Sudoku

Complete the grid so that each row, each column and each 3 x 3 frame contains the nine letters from the black box below. The hidden nine-letter word is in the diagonal from top left to bottom right.

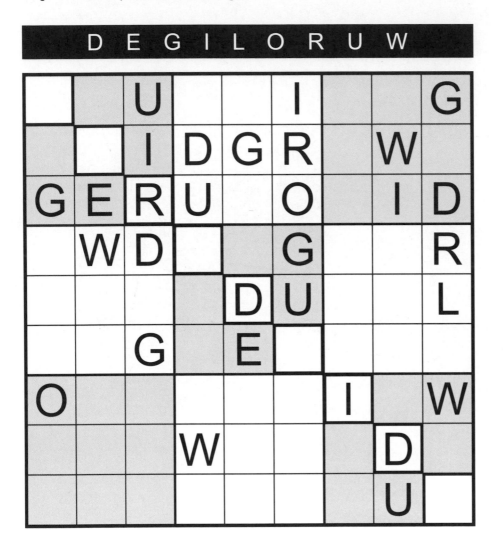

UNCANNY TURN

Rearrange the letters of the phrase below to form a cognate anagram, one which is related or connected in meaning to the original phrase. The answer can be one or more words.

ON TIP

★ Binairo

Complete the grid with zeros and ones until there are 5 zeros and 6 ones in every row and every column. No more than two of the same number can be next to or under each other. Rows or columns with exactly the same content are not allowed. There is only one valid solution.

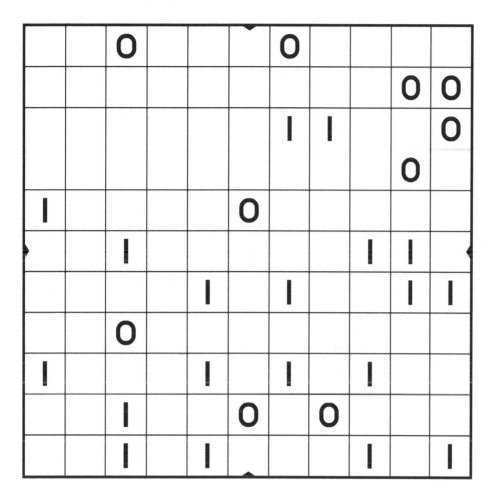

SANDWICH

What four-letter word belongs between the word on the left and the word on the right, so that the first and second word, and the second and third word, each form a common compound word or phrase?

HAND _ _ _ _ ABLE

★★ Stormy Weather by Michele Sayer

ACROSS

1 Serb, e.g.
5 Hard to deal with
10 Store safely
14 Prefix for "scope"
15 Bellybutton type
16 Cronyn in *Lifeboat*
17 Goes to a restaurant
18 Asian river and range
19 Lombardy Castle city
20 1990 A-ha hit
23 Mother's hermana
24 Cutup
25 Starbucks worker
29 Expert with a joystick
33 Once more, in Dogpatch
34 One may be seen on a model
36 Before, to Keats
37 1952 Debbie Reynolds film
41 Game stew meat
42 What Grafton's "N" stands for
43 Under sail
44 Purifies, in a way
46 Zinc-carbon battery
49 Shania Twain hit
50 "A mouse!"
51 2000 Enya album
60 Make espresso
61 High times
62 River through the Czech Republic
63 Theda of silent films
64 Pre-meal recitation
65 Terrible twos responses
66 Words on some cigars
67 Sometimes they battle
68 Primer

DOWN

1 Many authors write on it
2 *All in the Family* producer
3 Dilettantish
4 Calling on
5 Snickers ingredient
6 Ear: Prefix
7 Shaw in *Fried Green Tomatoes*
8 Pinball term
9 Rabbinical seminary
10 Native of Himalayan slopes
11 Fish in a casserole
12 Futuristic magazine
13 Gradually withdraw (from)
21 Birthplace of Constantine the Great
22 Hirsch in *The Emperor's Club*
25 Working (out of)
26 Twinkle-toed
27 Places for curlers
28 "So long, Sancho!"
29 Feigned
30 Pester
31 Window for plants
32 Near the kidneys
35 Some dashes
38 Acquired relative
39 Whisper sweet ____
40 Greedy landlord's income
45 "Nevertheless ..."
47 Utilizes a hand-me-down
48 Eventually
51 "Fernando" group
52 Humdrum
53 Designed to minimize wind resistance
54 Put a rip in
55 Paul is dead, e.g.
56 It's enough, according to some
57 Emollient ingredient
58 Mountain goat
59 Wren's dwelling

★ Cage the Animals

Draw lines to completely divide up the grid into small squares with exactly one animal per square. The squares should not overlap.

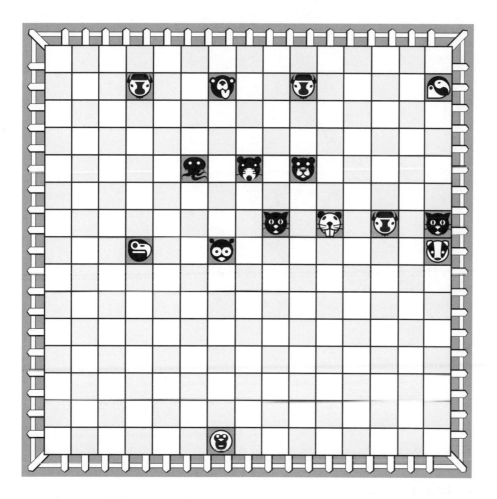

WORD WALL

Beginning at the left side of the wall, make a word by adding one group of letters from each column as you move left to right. When you have found the first word, go back to the second column and start the next word, gathering one group of letters from each column, and so on until all the letters are used to make six words.

★★ BrainSnack®—Spokes

The final sprint will be won by rider number 2 followed by riders 1, 6, 10, 3, 9 etc. Which rider will be last?

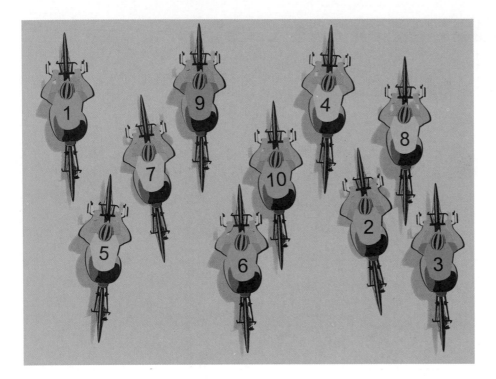

QUICK WORD SEARCH

Find the musical terms listed below in the word search grid.

```
O V E R T U R E C I T A L E F
C A R O L E R U S A E M T M I
K O C T A V E W Q U A R T E T
U N I S O N E C N E D A C H O
R E F R A I N A T U R A L T M
```

CADENCE QUARTET CAROL RECITAL MEASURE REFRAIN MOTIF
THEME NATURAL UNISON OCTAVE OVERTURE

★★ Hoofers by Maggie Ellis

ACROSS

1 Sew with an egg
5 Snopes subject
9 Cossack's weapon
14 Canal to Oneida Lake
15 Mr. Saarinen
16 Shy of a treaty
17 *Sugar Babies* dancer
19 Exorcised
20 FBI head?
21 Mighty mount
23 "Seventh ___": Johnny Rivers
24 Correct a key problem?
27 Mattress coils
31 Artisans in clay
32 Thereby
33 Like some seals
35 Like ___ out of hell
36 Emblem of sovereignty
37 Impertinence
38 MTA stop
39 Installs carpeting
41 "___ porridge hot ..."
43 Pickled root
44 Edmonton football team
46 Hardly mild
48 Liam who voiced Aslan
49 Lupine lair
50 Piece for the piano
52 Ricocheted
56 Monica of tennis
58 *Singin' in the Rain* dancer
60 Crystal-gazers
61 Pâté de foie ___
62 4-point H, e.g.
63 Unlike filibusters
64 Pre-college exams
65 *The Wind in the Willows* hero

DOWN

1 Heedless
2 *The Temple of Dullness* composer
3 Orange zest source
4 Ness vis-à-vis Capone
5 Jumble
6 Team booster
7 Three, in Roma
8 ___ d'oeuvres
9 Concourse
10 Short operatic piece
11 *Broadway Melody of 1938* dancer
12 Prefix for sphere
13 One whistling at athletes
18 Rustable metal
22 Stomped
25 Jabbers on
26 Waugh's Brideshead, e.g.
27 Purloined
28 Expression
29 *42nd Street* dancer
30 Gross receipts
31 Gatorade parent
34 Sea inlet
40 *Hannah and Her ___* (1986)
41 Swimming hole
42 Lasting forever
43 "Just in Time" singer Tony
45 Creamy dessert
47 Boat wood
51 Clutch in a coop
52 Black fly
53 Ad writer's honor
54 Jazz giant Fitzgerald
55 Colored artificially
56 Rapid transport of yore
57 Wide shoe width
59 NOW objective, once

★ Garden

All the words are hidden vertically, horizontally or diagonally—in both directions. The letters that remain unused form a sentence from left to right.

```
A H E R B G A R D E N L L O P
T M E N T S C N R O M E I R N
G R E E N D A E I R F F U S E
P R E C N S P T E S O N R T T
A W S N R E A N N D E S H C T
T A A P E O E E O S S I N E E
I T F R C D P L U X U D I S M
O E C O R P R R N N Y M G N P
P R V A U O E A O G E G U I E
L F G E T N T I G T A T E H R
A A B A L D T S E E A G T N A
N L W A N A R A O D L T E L T
T L N N T I S O I P R T I N E
D A M I E N C B T N M A S O L
L G D C L I M B E R A O R A N
O E E K A R D E N N S A C N C
M L A W N M O W E R C D R O C
K G A R D E D R O U G H T N S
```

GREEN
HERB GARDEN
HUMUS
INSECTS
LAWN
LAWN MOWER
MEDITATION
MOLD
NETTLE
ORGANIC
OXYGEN
PATIO PLANT
POND
PRUNE
RAKE
SAND
TEMPERATE
WATERFALL

BENCH
CASTLE GARDEN
CLIMBER

COMPOST
CREEPER
CROP ROTATION

DROUGHT
FOUNTAIN
GARDENER

DELETE ONE

Delete one letter from A FLARING END and reach the climax.

★★ Futoshiki

Fill in the 5 x 5 grid with the numbers from 1 to 5 once per row and column, while following the greater than/lesser than symbols shown. There is only one valid solution that can be reached through logic and clear thinking alone!

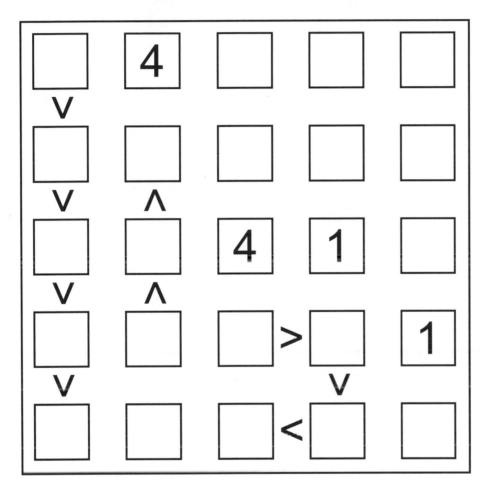

LETTERBLOCKS

Move the letterblocks around so that words are formed on top and below that you can associate with war.

★★ Hard Stuff by Tim Wagner

ACROSS

1 College mil. program
5 Letter after rho
10 Like two peas in ___
14 Con ___ (spiritedly)
15 Diet guru Jenny
16 Tackle box item
17 "Holy Smoke" band
19 Federal law officer
20 Hustler in *The Hustler*
21 *Beatles for Sale* song
23 Rickles zinger
26 Femme's husband
27 Venomous snake
29 Makes conscious (of)
32 Molding style
33 Novarro of silent films
35 *The Morning Watch*
   novelist
36 "As if, laddie!"
37 Male swan
38 "___ had better days"
39 Steve Harvey column
   "Only ___"
41 Union Pacific stop
43 Derby projection
44 Wranglers
46 1979 Janis Joplin
   biopic
48 *Laugh-In* giggler
49 Came down
50 Outstanding, as a
   performance
53 Goalie's glove
54 Mars: Comb. form
55 Superman's sobriquet
60 Ceramics oven
61 Not merely sluggish
62 Impose a tax on
63 ___ dixit (no proof
   needed)
64 Subtly mean
65 Exuberance

DOWN

1 Stat for a Dodger
2 Bruin Hall-of-Famer
3 Nadal's uncle
4 Prove wrong
5 Disperse
6 Six-petaled flower
7 Type of fly
8 Way of carrying
   oneself
9 Additional name
10 Batna's country
11 Bodybuilding film of
   1977
12 Said aloud
13 Make a
   counterstatement
18 Promenade
22 Bighorn male
23 Double-edged

24 1998 Olympics site
25 1989 Rolling Stones
   album
28 Track events
29 Auto plant worker
30 Think up
31 Appeared
34 Disheveled hair
40 Large sea snail
41 Vigorous
42 Prudent with one's
   resources
43 Liable to crack
45 Minerva's symbol
47 Din-din
50 Hector Hugh Munro's
   pen name
51 Fall cause
52 Frog genus
53 Publisher Zuckerman

56 Bottom-line figure
57 Wiggling fish
58 Mendes in *The Women*
59 Indy racer St. James

★ Spot the Differences

Find the nine differences in the image on the right.

DOODLE PUZZLE

A doodle puzzle is a combination of images, letters and/or numbers that represent a word or a concept. If you cannot solve a doodle puzzle, do not look at the answer right away. Think hard—and outside the box.

f@f.ff

★★ BrainSnack®—Big Game

Which numbers should replace the question marks?

LETTER LINE

Put a letter in each of the squares below to make a word which is much in evidence. The number clues refer to other words which can be made from the whole.

8 2 3 7 1 4 5 OF PLANTS OR PLANT LIFE;
8 7 9 5 2 1 10 EXTENDING PLATFORM;
1 2 3 7 8 9 6 WORTHY OF ATTENTION OR NOTICE;
1 2 8 9 6 OF HIGH RANK; 8 2 7 3 WATER TRANSPORT

1	2	3	4	5	6	7	8	9	10

★★ High Spirits by Tim Wagner

ACROSS

1 Melville whaler
5 Die
10 Spice Girls hit
14 *Avatar* humanoids
15 Pews divider
16 Facetious "I see"
17 Donald L. Coburn play
19 Film unit
20 Heroin, on the street
21 Wardrobe
23 Chops finely
26 *Star Trek* navigator
27 Ones providing arms?
29 Thorny problem
32 Oodles
33 ___ Bell (Anne Brontë)
35 Author LeShan and others
36 Soak flax
37 Weed out
38 Winning candidates
39 Faction within a faith
41 Truffles et al.
43 Wife of a rajah
44 Joseph's second son
46 Concert bonuses
48 Comedienne Roseanne
49 1981 royal wedding figure
50 Mocks or knocks
53 Judi Dench, for one
54 Stratford-___-Avon
55 Colorful Kentucky turkey
60 Wee bit
61 Heavens: Comb. form
62 "Big Yellow ___": Joni Mitchell
63 Motrin target
64 Eva in *Gigi*
65 Main part of a word

DOWN

1 Pismire
2 "Pfft! Right!"
3 "Greetings, Caesar!"
4 Pooh bah
5 Multi-deck game
6 Diana of *The Avengers*
7 Mama bear in Marbella
8 ___ mater
9 Constrains
10 Hilshire Farm parent
11 2011 Johnny Depp film
12 Hosea, in the Douay Bible
13 Trend determiner
18 NHL penalty killer
22 Afghan coin
23 Funeral car
24 In slumberland
25 Barley soup
28 Rugby action
29 Avoid artfully
30 Staffed
31 Home of St. Francis
34 A base metal
40 Recent hire
41 Pyromaniac
42 About to deliver
43 Chipmunk and squirrel, e.g.
45 Suffix for drunk
47 Hunting wear, for short
50 ___ *Key*: Stephen King
51 Of historic dimensions
52 Common rail
53 Bond baddie with a base on Crab Key
56 Birmingham college
57 Nick in *Chicken Run*
58 Program file extension
59 Barely lit

★ Safe Code

To open the safe you have to replace the question mark with the correct figure. You can find this figure by determining the logical method behind the numbers shown. These methods can include calculation, inversion, repetition, chronological succession, or forming ascending and descending series.

SAFE A08

SANDWICH

What five-letter word belongs between the word on the left and the word on the right, so that the first and second word, and the second and third word, each form a common compound word or phrase?

PAINT _ _ _ _ _ WOOD

★ Word Pyramid

Each word in the pyramid has the letters of the word above it, plus a new letter.

S
(1) direction
(2) group of things
(3) shelter made by a bird
(4) rear part of a ship
(5) put in
(6) cocktail of crème de menthe and brandy
(7) whole numbers

DOUBLETALK

Homophones are words that share the same pronunciation, no matter how they are spelled.
If they are spelled differently then they are called heterographs. Find heterographs meaning:

TO WALK IN WATER and MEASURED

★★ Sudoku

Fill in the grid so that each row, each column and each 3 x 3 frame contains every number from 1 to 9.

				5				
					2	4		
	3						5	
2								
			2		6	5		8
	5		4	9	3		6	
4				7		6		
8				2	1		9	4
9	6		8	4			1	2

SYMBOL SUMS

Can you work out these number sums using three of these four symbols? **+ − ÷ ×**
(No fractions or minus numbers are involved in the sum as you progress from left to right.)

$$19 \ \square \ 3 \ \square \ 2 \ \square \ 3 = 24$$

★★★ Rita and Company by John M. Samson

ACROSS

1 Woody Allen film feature
6 Maryam in *The Living Daylights*
10 Glittery mineral
14 Silty river feature
15 "Got ___ named Daisy ..."
16 Jimmy Buffett's "Son of ___ of a Sailor"
17 Steer away from
18 Rita's *Only Angels Have Wings* costar
20 Sea cow
22 Follow suit
23 No, in Russian
24 Sticker figures
25 Perdition
28 Oven used for firing ceramics
29 Cross
30 Israeli coin
32 Partially opened
36 Debussy's *La ___*
37 Scooby-___
38 Italian gold
39 Gucci of design
41 "Bleeding Love" singer Lewis
43 An Everly brother
44 Stratagem
46 Arms depot
48 Steak-au-poivre seasoning
51 Spring event
52 C-worthy
54 Playground planks
57 Rita's *Cover Girl* costar
59 Unwaveringly true
60 Diving eagles
61 Body's largest organ
62 Épée attack
63 Hides the gray
64 Champagne head?
65 Quickness

DOWN

1 Baldwin in *The Patriot*
2 St. Petersburg river
3 Rita's *Gilda* costar
4 Deviated
5 Rip to pieces
6 Bait fish
7 Turkish general
8 Adriatic seaport
9 Dukakis in *Moonstruck*
10 Country singer McBride
11 Asimov or Stern
12 Richard in *The Godfather*
13 Builds a pot
19 "The ___ From Ipanema"
21 Sicilian volcano
25 Rombauer of cookery
26 Yule tune
27 City near Great Salt Lake
28 Swedish coin
31 New odometer setting
33 Rita's *Circus World* star
34 Prima donna's song
35 Frank holder
40 Put under the yoke
41 Bigger than the rest
42 Jester Johnson
43 Green appetizer
45 Security breach
47 Nut cases
48 Called in an airport
49 ___ man jack
50 Tubular pasta
53 Actress Sommer
54 "... for auld lang ___"
55 Salary
56 It goes downhill fast
58 Illumined

★★ Keep Going

Start on a blank square of your choice and connect as many blank squares as possible with one single continuous line. You can only connect squares along vertical and horizontal lines. You must continue the connecting line up until the next obstacle, i.e., the rim of the box, a black square or a square that has already been used. You can change direction at any obstacle you meet. Each square can be used only once. The number of blank squares that will be left unused is marked in the upper square. There is more than one solution. We show only one solution.

FRIENDS?

What do the following words have in common?

RANGER MASTER FIRES WHACK LANDS

★★ BrainSnack®—At the Movies

Which number is missing on the last theater ticket?

WORD WALL

Beginning at the left side of the wall, make a word by adding one group of letters from each column as you move left to right. When you have found the first word, go back to the second column and start the next word, gathering one group of letters from each column, and so on until all the letters are used to make six words.

★★★ Scrap Heap by Karen Peterson

ACROSS

1 Study hard
5 Partners of starts
9 Former TV host Philbin
14 Hägar the Horrible's daughter
15 Genus of olives
16 Military storehouse
17 Carbo-loads
18 Brook
19 Midnight blue
20 Weigh-in insults
22 Tree
23 Note from an unlucky gambler
24 Winona's *Dracula* role
25 1981 werewolf film (with *The*)
29 Desert illusions
32 Botanical wings
33 Blunder
35 Security concern
36 Birth certificates, e.g.
37 Thun's river
38 "... man ___ mouse?"
39 Pickled cheese
41 Early anesthetic
43 Cock-and-___ story
44 Buttercup relative
46 Tracked down
48 Missing
49 Small island
50 Steep slope
52 High-risk securities
58 Blackman in *Goldfinger*
59 Away from the wind
60 *Snow Crash* author Stephenson
61 Provide, as with some quality
62 Stun gun missile
63 Greek war goddess
64 Disheveled
65 Peyton Manning targets
66 Trial balloon

DOWN

1 Hardy Boys pal Morton
2 Emulate Leo
3 Architectural pier
4 Airborne weapon
5 Fame's companion
6 Olympic skater Kulik
7 Narrate
8 Polio vaccine developer
9 Do a tinker's job
10 Endless
11 Part of GIGO
12 ___ facto (as an inevitable result)
13 Tea-leaf reader
21 ___ polloi
24 "Peace" space station
25 Seaport in Israel
26 Of the past
27 Moors
28 Gas-grill part
29 Sponge mushroom
30 "Some Dreams" singer Steve
31 Old Scandinavian bard
34 Loud cheer
40 In the mood
41 Tolkien forest giant
42 Houston hoopsters
43 Rifle adjunct
45 Sea hawk
47 Urban ride
50 Noah's eldest son
51 Orange road marker
52 Green gem
53 ___ Bator, Mongolia
54 Techie type
55 Brazil NBA star
56 "Thirty ___ hath ..."
57 Open position

★ Cooking Techniques

All the words are hidden vertically, horizontally or diagonally—in both directions. The letters that remain unused form a sentence from left to right.

```
H T H E V E R P R E S E R V E
S B M U R C D A E R B U B T O
U C O A H O K G E I I S A A C
R O E C R L N L N P U R E U L
C E A X C I B D I N O T A I L
V O E R T M N C T A I E U R L
P B A L E I K A S M F A G A I
O E A S R L N T T A L M R L K
S S S K E T G G H E A D A T S
K A E W E A R Y U E S T T C S
C H A T R E I F T I O O I O T
O D C E U A L S N B S E N O N
T P V D E G L A Z E R H E K E
S O N K B L A N C H P A R E M
C O O K U N T I L D O N E R R
F M E N P A P I L L O T E Y E
S G R I N D Y R F P E E D E F
E U C E B R A B B R A I S E D
```

COOKERY
COVER
CRUSH
DEEP FRY
DEGLAZE
EN PAPILLOTE
EXTINGUISH
FERMENT
FONDUE
GRILL
GRIND
LARD
LUAU
MARINATE
PICKLE
POACH
PRESERVE
PURE
ROAST
SALTING
SEAR
SKILL
SMOKE
STEAM
STOCK
STRAIN

ASSEMBLE
AU GRATIN
BAKE
BARBECUE
BIND
BLANCH
BRAISE
BREADCRUMBS
COOK UNTIL DONE

DELETE ONE

Delete one letter from SAD TIN TEETH and find someone who can help.

★★★ Sport Maze

Draw the shortest way from the ball to the goal. You can only move along vertical and horizontal lines, not along diagonal lines. The figure on each square indicates the number of squares the ball must be moved in the same direction. You can change direction at each stop.

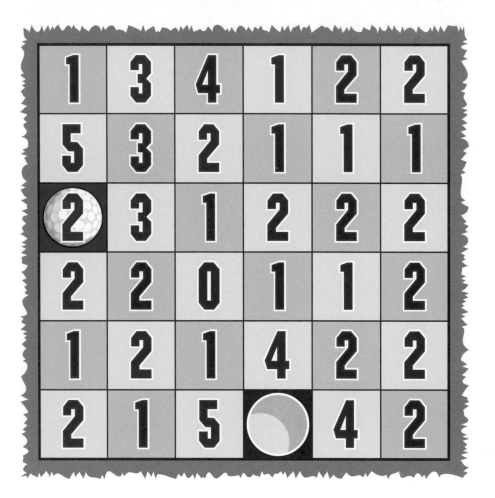

ONE LETTER LESS OR MORE

The word on the right side contains the letters of the word on the left side plus or minus the letter in the middle. One letter is already in the right place.

★★★ **The Odd Trio** by Mary Leonard

ACROSS

1 Foal's mom
5 Smug moralists
10 Angelic glow
14 Prominent periods
15 100 kopeks
16 Between
17 Grammy winner ___ Anthony
18 Hamburger topper
19 Not a lick
20 Mohegan Sun machines
23 Baby food
24 ___ Aviv
25 They're brilliant
29 Fodder sack
33 Pre-owned
34 Standard and ___ Index
36 Old Tokyo
37 1978 Commodores hit
41 Alert color
42 Kidney enzyme
43 Epithet of Athena
44 Safari sightings
46 Choreographed ones
49 Worked on a sub
50 Neither's partner
51 The Vogues hit of 1965
60 Norse war god
61 Concerning the ears
62 Char
63 Spanish stewpot
64 Labor feverishly
65 *Buona* ___, *Mrs. Campbell* (1968)
66 Like Lucy's red hair
67 Melodies
68 Swirling water

DOWN

1 Office missive
2 Flaherty's *Man of* ___
3 Far from frequent
4 Janet Jackson hit
5 On time
6 Viking letter
7 "The same" in footnotes
8 Serving of whipped cream
9 Ottawa NHL team
10 Doorknob
11 Mine, in Montmartre
12 Laundry residue
13 Poems of praise
21 Migrated upstream, as salmon
22 Holt of *Las Vegas*
25 Buddhist sermon
26 Pasty

27 *La Traviata* composer
28 Twirls about
29 Immensely
30 Memphis blues street
31 Calculating one?
32 "The Naked Maja" and "The Clothed Maja"
35 Lake of Japan
38 Muse of Greek myth
39 Put on the air
40 Native American sport, originally
45 Priestess of Dionysus
47 Bobbysocks reach them
48 At once
51 Comestibles
52 Stand ___ by
53 Offensive
54 "To Sir, With Love" singer

55 Algerian port
56 Stalactite site
57 Panpipe
58 Overlay with bacon
59 Low cart

★★ Word Sudoku

Complete the grid so that each row, each column and each 3 x 3 frame contains the nine letters from the black box below. The hidden nine-letter word is in the diagonal from top left to bottom right.

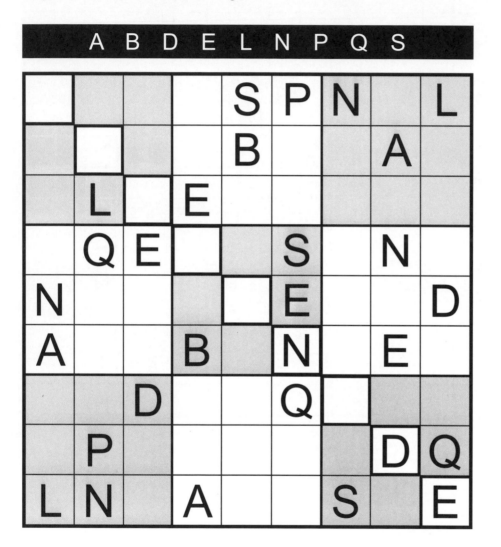

A	B	D	E	L	N	P	Q	S

				S	P	N		L
				B			A	
	L		E					
	Q	E			S		N	
N					E			D
A			B		N		E	
		D			Q			
	P						D	Q
L	N		A			S		E

UNCANNY TURN

Rearrange the letters of the phrase below to form a cognate anagram, one which is related or connected in meaning to the original phrase. The answer can be one or more words.

STRONGER AS SINS

★★ Sudoku X

Fill in the grid so that each row, each column and each 3 x 3 frame contains every number from 1 to 9. The two main diagonals of the grid also contain every number from 1 to 9.

		4	2		1		7	8
	2		7		6			3
			8		4		1	
9	5			7				
1				6			3	7
	8				9		6	
		9					2	
2								
	6					5		

BLOCK ANAGRAM

Form the words that are described in the brackets with the letters above the grid. Extra letters are already in the right place.

GOLDMATTERS (skin doctor)

★★★ On an Even Keel by Mary Leonard

ACROSS

- **1** Tool booth
- **5** Google service
- **10** Spread out
- **14** Hercules fell in love with her
- **15** Needing practice
- **16** Equine hybrid
- **17** 1962 Mitchum/MacLaine film
- **20** Disaffect
- **21** Italics trait
- **22** Court dividers
- **23** Slopes upward
- **25** Gidget portrayer Dee
- **28** Play at love
- **29** Siouan
- **30** Heavenly combiner
- **31** Arrange type
- **34** Ian Tyson folk song
- **38** "AP" of India
- **39** CNN anchor Burnett et al.
- **40** "Dungeons & Dragons" spirit
- **41** Massive
- **42** Soho cig
- **44** Update
- **47** Cufflink's spot
- **48** Betelgeuse locale
- **49** Andalusian
- **53** Thoroughly
- **56** "6 'N the Mornin' " rapper
- **57** "Double Stuf" cookies
- **58** "The ___ of Amontillado": Poe
- **59** *A Beautiful Mind* subject
- **60** Insignificant
- **61** Apple or cherry

DOWN

- **1** ___ spell (rest)
- **2** Riot
- **3** *The Time Machine* fruit eaters
- **4** One who provides protection
- **5** Flubs
- **6** Junkyard dogs
- **7** NYC's Arthur ___ Stadium
- **8** Kin of -ian
- **9** Ghent river
- **10** Breakfast order
- **11** Korean War beachhead site
- **12** Serengeti animal
- **13** Salamanders
- **18** Nonesuch
- **19** Money held in trust
- **23** Alda and King
- **24** Tattle
- **25** Like a slow market
- **26** Whole lots
- **27** Verb's subject
- **28** Weather-map line
- **30** Bathsheba's husband
- **31** Lose control
- **32** U2 guitarist The ___
- **33** Boris Godunov, e.g.
- **35** *Gossip Girl* girl
- **36** "___ bien!"
- **37** Doing what comes naturally
- **41** Mutual-fund objective
- **42** Glazed, as eyes
- **43** Japanese ethnic group
- **44** Pitcher's aid
- **45** *All My Children* role
- **46** Tight spots
- **47** CIA operative, slangily
- **49** Compact Chevy pickup
- **50** Jewish month before Nisan
- **51** Demolish, in Ontario
- **52** Flood prevention
- **54** Hebrew "Y"
- **55** ___ Lanka

★★ BrainSnack®—Web of Intrigue

The yellow zones are closely monitored by the spider. Which zone (1–13) should also be yellow?

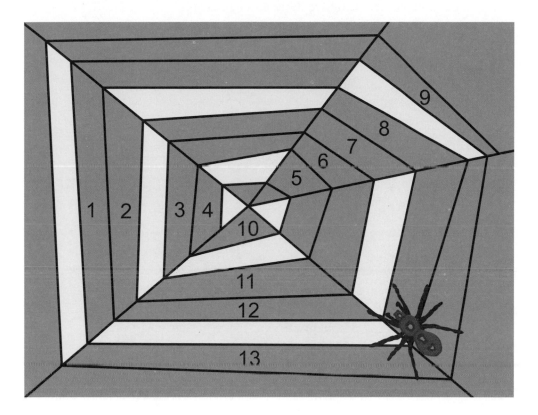

QUICK CROSSWORD

Place the words listed below in the crossword grid.

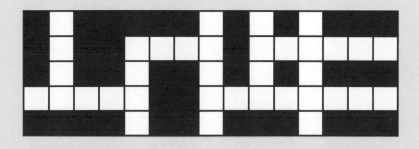

BRIO BODY VERVE ENERGY BLOOD ACTIVITY ZEST WOMAN SOUL

★★ Sunny Weather

Where will the sun shine? With the knowledge that each arrow points to
a place where a symbol should be, can you locate the sunny spots? The
symbols cannot be next to each other vertically, horizontally or diagonally.
A symbol cannot be placed on top of an arrow. We show one symbol.

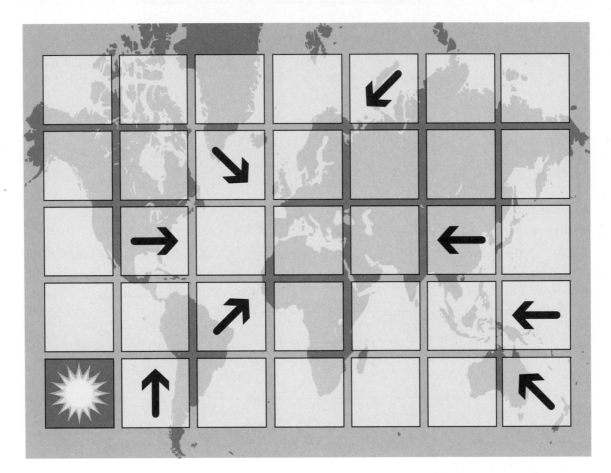

TRIANAGRAM

Three-word groups of anagrams are also called triplets or trianagrams.
Complete the group:

DESERT _ _ _ _ _ _   _ _ _ _ _ _

★★★ Suit Cases by Don Law

ACROSS

1 Company VIP: Abbr.
5 Sunbathe
9 Midway attractions
14 Houston hockey pro
15 Off-Broadway award
16 De Becque in *South Pacific*
17 Preparatory research
19 Skoal or prosit
20 Completely
21 Mysteries
23 Food from a tropical tuber
24 Martian prefix
25 Parrot's forte
29 Pass at Innsbruck
32 Like some pockets
33 "___ be!"
35 Contrary flow
36 Stage great Hagen
37 Victorian ___
38 Kettle cover
39 Where the sidewalk ends
41 Payload
43 What a stitch saves
44 "1-2-3" singer Gloria
46 Star pupil
48 Juvenile
49 Monkey suit
50 One who gets physical
53 Rational
57 Sword of Damocles
58 19th hole
60 Mâcon's river
61 Russo in *Big Trouble*
62 Beekeeper of film
63 Fireplace glower
64 ___-friendly
65 Hexagram

DOWN

1 Bygone
2 Recovered car
3 Part of QED
4 Designated driver's drink
5 Alley sport
6 "___ Named Sue"
7 Celtic god of the sea
8 Palmer in *Joyful Noise*
9 Call it a day
10 Comic Coca
11 Broadway play by Mae West
12 Soprano role in *Lohengrin*
13 Stops the bidder
18 Beautiful Wells race
22 ___ a soul
25 Reason out
26 The Whale constellation
27 Matinee idol
28 Find out, in a way
29 Crows
30 Jennifer Saunders role
31 Winona in *Mr. Deeds*
34 Benjamin of the Cars
40 Direct route
41 Quilter's word
42 *The Hunt for Red ___* (1990)
43 Unhealthy
45 Trial balloon
47 Wolverine player Jackman
50 It's often vaulted
51 Sleigh pullers
52 Restate in agreement
53 *Clair de ___*: Debussy
54 Jim Jones led one
55 Under sail
56 Suggestive look
59 Guitar master Paul

★★ Kakuro

Each number in a black area is the sum of the numbers that you have to enter in the next empty boxes. The empty boxes that make up the sum are called a run. The sum of the across run is written above the diagonal in the black area and the sum of the down run is written below the diagonal. Runs can only contain the numbers 1 through 9 and each number in a run can only be used once. The gray boxes only contain odd numbers and the white only even numbers.

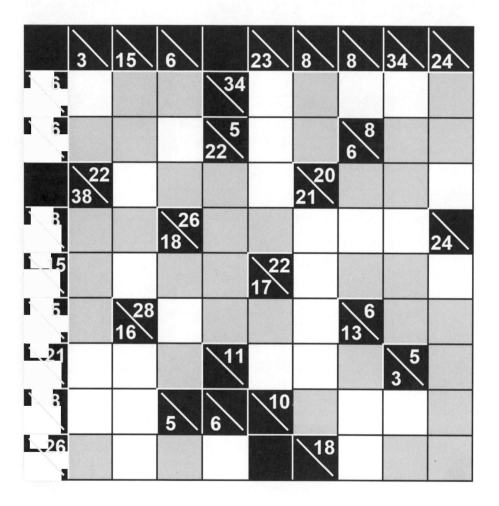

DOUBLETALK

Homophones are words that share the same pronunciation, no matter how they are spelled. If they are spelled differently then they are called heterographs. Find heterographs meaning:

A TABLE OF DAYS and MAKES PAPER SMOOTH

★★ Sudoku Twin

Fill in the grid so that each row, each column and each 3 x 3 frame contains every number from 1 to 9. A sudoku twin is two connected 9 x 9 sudokus.

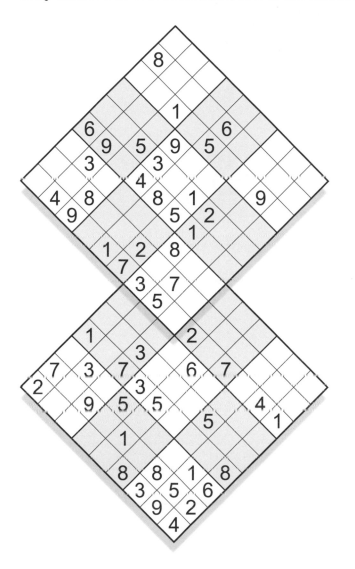

TRIANAGRAM

Three-word groups of anagrams are also called triplets or trianagrams.
Complete the group:

ARCHES _ _ _ _ _ _   _ _ _ _ _ _

★★ BrainSnack®—Beach Days

What temperature should replace the question mark?

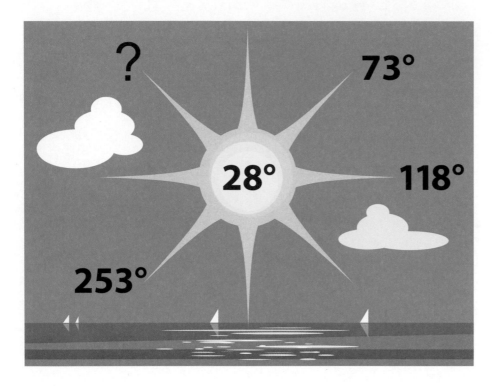

CHANGELINGS

Each of the three lines of letters below spell words which relate to meetings, but the letters have been mixed up. Four letters from the first word are now in the third line, four letters from the third word are in the second line and four letters from the second word are in the first line. The remaining letters are in their original places. What are the words?

P R A U N S T V R E
G E R S M A S I N T
A B R E E I E O M S

★★★ The Elements by Don Law

ACROSS

1 College mil. program
5 *Rocky IV* heavy
10 Rock to sleep
14 Crossword cookie
15 Sniggler
16 Rapier's cousin
17 Dynamic person
19 Pickle
20 Jumper's lack
21 2002 Christina Ricci film
23 *A Few Good ___* (1992)
24 Pocket fuzz
25 Kerry's 2004 running mate
29 Prohibition prohibition
32 Novelist Updike
33 Impudent
35 Campbell in *Scream*
36 Ambient rocker Brian
37 Temper tantrum
38 NYC-based insurance corp.
39 Songsmith Porter
41 Roaming free
43 Super Bowl prize
44 Lattice
46 Idolizes
48 Sparkle
49 Big cheese
50 Rolling grassland
53 Apian way
57 Galley needs
58 City W of Tampa
60 Director Preminger
61 Kunta of *Roots*
62 Briton or Gaul
63 Violinist Hilary
64 Brewing agent
65 Oilman Halliburton

DOWN

1 Burgles
2 Viva voce
3 Prefix for scope
4 Dabney in *On Golden Pond*
5 Shields
6 Fight stoppers
7 "Greatest" boxer
8 Microbe
9 *Culture Warrior* author
10 Beirut locale
11 Uncertain
12 ___ a hand
13 Spartan queen of myth
18 Communication closer
22 *New York* director Burns
25 DVD-player button
26 Blood-bank depositor
27 Stewart Brand's *Catalog*
28 Repositories
29 "When You Wish Upon ___"
30 Sheepish
31 Pantyhose brand
34 Mick Jagger's title
40 Oracle founder Larry
41 Like some eaters
42 Young hare
43 Supplant
45 Park-Lincoln of *Knots Landing*
47 Vista
50 Piglet's pal
51 ___-tat-tat
52 Peace Nobelist Wiesel
53 Baseball Hall of Fame sights
54 Roman road
55 Little Dickens girl
56 "Symphony in "Black" artist
59 *Bambi* aunt

★ Construction

All the words are hidden vertically, horizontally or diagonally—in both directions. The letters that remain unused form a sentence from left to right.

```
T H E C O N C S F M T R U C T
I R S T E E L O T T O O N I N
D E U S M T R C C R Y R I S A
P M N E E E E R A C O T N D
L O N O M J T E M E B P I A U
A T C A O I N C P C S L E C R
S S N R H G E I T O O A E R A
T U P C I W P T S L T N H S B
E C R S O N R S E O A N T F L
R A E O I O A A G G C E U S E
E D D A T E C L D Y S R O N M
R A R K I C N P I O F F I C E
G D H O M E A S R O O F E R W
A G R A V E L R B R I C K N I
D O N A I C I R T C E L E T R
T N E M N O R I V N E H E R I
R E B M U L P S T R O U C T N
S L A I R E T A M U R C E S G
```

DRAINPIPE
DURABLE
ECOLOGY
ELECTRICIAN
ENVIRONMENT
FOREMAN
GRAVEL
MATERIALS
MORTAR
OFFICE
PLANNER
PLASTERER
PLASTIC
PLUMBER
PROJECT
ROOFER
STEEL
WIRING
WOOD

ARCHITECT
BRICK
BRIDGES

CABLES
CARPENTER
CEMENT

CONTRACTOR
CUSTOMER
DESIGNER

DELETE ONE

Delete one letter from CARES IF NOTED and do not cause inconvenience or hurt to others.

★ Hourglass

Starting in the middle, each word in the top half has the letters of the word below it, plus a new letter, and each word in the bottom half has the letters of the word above it, plus a new letter.

(1) looks up to
(2) stargazes
(3) stain with a dirty substance
(4) identical
(5) occasion for buying at reduced prices
(6) untrue
(7) fires
(8) women

UNCANNY TURN

Rearrange the letters of the phrase below to form a cognate anagram, one which is related or connected in meaning to the original phrase. The answer can be one or more words.

OH TO MAN GREAT AIDS

★★★ Hannah and Her Sisters by Linda Lather

ACROSS

1 Cowboy tie
5 Nose around
10 Rooney in *The Girl With the Dragon Tattoo*
14 Checking device
15 Kind of culture dish
16 Not quite yet
17 *Black Beauty* author
19 Little buzzer
20 Carl Sagan book
21 Honors
23 Extinguished
24 Pinta's sister ship
25 Compressed
29 Like a keystone
32 Sherbet holder
33 Gossip
35 Building lot
36 Footed vase
37 Big campaign donor
38 Kind of party
39 Podium
41 "The Lion and the Mouse" fabulist
43 Bit of headway
44 Erstwhile
46 Skier Tomba
48 Luxurious
49 Internet service provider
50 Abridge
53 Broaden
57 Jacques in *Mon Oncle*
58 Classic rag doll
60 Suffix for bachelor
61 Summer ermine
62 ___ *Almighty* (2007)
63 Kerfuffle
64 *Merrie Melodies* stars
65 Mountain ___ (sodas)

DOWN

1 Bric-a-___
2 Wine: Comb. form
3 *Before You Sleep* novelist Ullmann
4 Literary Nobelist France
5 Ghost
6 Slender amphibian
7 Suffix for Capri
8 Escutcheon border
9 Light lager
10 Purplish red
11 *Fatal Attraction* actress
12 Have itchy feet
13 Echidnas eat them
18 Israel's first king
22 Bronze component
25 Old Italian coin
26 Capone's archrival "Bugs"
27 *Designing Women* actress
28 Capital of India?
29 Rink drink
30 "Looks ___ everything"
31 Slowly, to Stravinsky
34 Bell and Rainey
40 Lies
41 Emily Dickinson's home
42 Solar System members
43 Like some flights
45 Novel ending
47 Daring
50 From ___ to stern
51 Despise
52 Brussels-based alliance
53 Archbishop of New York (2000–09)
54 Rhapsodize
55 Chew on a bone
56 Danube tributary
59 Schmaltz

★★ Keep Going

Start on a blank square of your choice and connect as many blank squares as possible with one single continuous line. You can only connect squares along vertical and horizontal lines. You must continue the connecting line up until the next obstacle, i.e., the rim of the box, a black square or a square that has already been used. You can change direction at any obstacle you meet. Each square can be used only once. The number of blank squares that will be left unused is marked in the upper square. There is more than one solution. We show only one solution.

FRIENDS?

What do the following words have in common?

ABLE ER BACK BOY USED

★★★ Sport Maze

Draw the shortest way from the ball to the goal. You can only move along
vertical and horizontal lines, not along diagonal lines. The figure on each square
indicates the number of squares the ball must be moved in the same direction.
You can change direction at each stop.

4	4	3	5	4	2
1	3	3	2	2	4
③	4	1	2	1	2
1	3	3	2	0	2
3	2	1	2	1	2
2	2	3	5	⊙	2

ONE LETTER LESS OR MORE

The word on the right side contains the letters of the word on the left side plus or minus the
letter in the middle. One letter is already in the right place.

C A N O E I N G +R [ ] G [ ][ ][ ][ ][ ][ ]

★★★ Postgame Show by Michele Sayer

ACROSS

1 What doers take
6 It's perpendicular to a threshold
10 Wild guess
14 Film producer Ponti
15 Facebook member
16 Remedy
17 Like some flu strains
18 Normandy city
19 *Harper's Bazaar* illustrator
20 XXX, for one
23 Bungle the job
24 Italian summer resort
25 Floor covers
28 Linen robe
31 Veil
35 Bill in a tip jar
36 Pansy genus
38 Airplane walkway
39 Reality show with weigh-ins
42 Digital watch brand
43 Cosmetics name
44 Keys album *Songs ___ Minor*
45 Fashion designer McCartney
47 Viscous resin
48 Rink in *Giant*
49 Sylvester's speech flaw
51 Rock's ___ Speedwagon
53 Draws
61 Foreign exchange premium
62 Egress
63 Loosen a knot
64 Aquatic bird
65 "Proud Mary" rocker Turner
66 Do a winter chore
67 Observes
68 Third son of the first man
69 1959 Ford model

DOWN

1 Improvise like Ella
2 Kipling's "Rikki-Tikki-___"
3 Stonestreet of *Modern Family*
4 Vehicle IDs
5 Submarine detector
6 ___ deserts
7 Apropos of
8 Donnybrook
9 Cleveland team
10 Possible outcome
11 Go left or right
12 Commedia dell'___
13 Tapster's draw
21 James Bond actor Daniel
22 Breathe in
25 College mil. programs
26 Flip your lid
27 Gaggle members
29 Box seat
30 Hallowed, old-style
32 Davis in *Gladiator*
33 Suffix for fraud
34 Rid of vermin
36 Luthier's instrument
37 Skippy's *Thin Man* role
40 Huge amounts
41 ___ firma
46 Plusses
48 Wedded
50 Impish sort
52 Chopin genre
53 Washington team
54 S-shape curve
55 Electrician's supply
56 Hair enhancer
57 Mormon State
58 *Barnyard* bull
59 Chagall Museum site
60 Blind a falcon

★★ BrainSnack®—Drink Up!

The more Belgian beers you order, the cheaper they become. What is the price of the last beer?

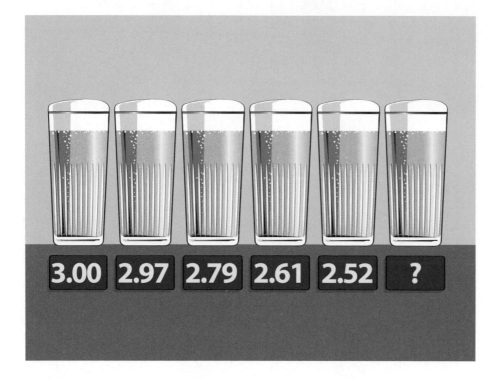

LETTER LINE

Put a letter in each of the squares below to make a word which is won back. The number clues refer to other words which can be made from the whole.

3 4 5 2 1 2 10 SCAMPERED; 6 2 1 1 4 3 2 10 WITH AN OPEN AREA OR WALKWAY; 8 9 6 1 4 3 2 10 GONE BACK OVER AGAIN; 6 1 7 2 HONEST; 9 8 7 5 6 OUTPOUR SUDDENLY

1	2	3	4	5	6	7	8	9	10

★★ Word Sudoku

Complete the grid so that each row, each column and each 3 x 3 frame contains the nine letters from the black box below. The hidden nine-letter word is in the diagonal from top left to bottom right.

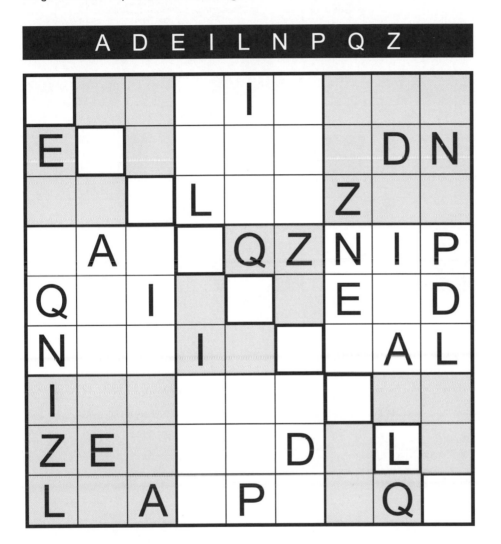

A D E I L N P Q Z

UNCANNY TURN

Rearrange the letters of the phrase below to form a cognate anagram, one which is related or connected in meaning to the original phrase. The answer can be one or more words.

THIRTY ROOMED

★★★ End Rhyme by Tim Wagner

ACROSS

1 Unit of matter
5 Doral Resort owner
10 Lecture locale
14 Corporate image
15 Running water
16 Pinza of opera
17 Shoulder injury
20 Former
21 Uniform ornament
22 Agent
23 Scepter topper
24 Became tangled
28 Elephant species
32 Puzzler's favorite ox
33 Up with the sun
35 Man ___ mission
36 Caprine fairy-tale triad
40 Marshland
41 Slutskaya of skating
42 Douay Bible book
43 Stymied
45 Ranters
48 Apple core?
49 West in *She Done Him Wrong*
50 Bickering
54 Musses
58 Demanded proof
60 Wicked
61 Saw-toothed
62 *Rent-___* (1988)
63 Coming-out girls
64 Income for Fred and Ethel Mertz
65 Scotland ___

DOWN

1 Jimmy Dorsey's sax
2 Bullwinkle, for one
3 Barbarous person
4 Cultural center of Quebec
5 ___ l'oeil (optical illusion)
6 Baptism, e.g.
7 Tanning ray
8 Dole (out)
9 Pops the question
10 Priam's wife
11 Blue, in Brazil
12 Milton Bradley board game
13 Soho apartment
18 Cambodian's 100 sen
19 ___ to go (eager)
24 Yeshiva instructor
25 Charged particle
26 Europe's longest river
27 "Dieu et mon ___" (royal English motto)
28 "When You Wish Upon ___"
29 Put ___ (employ)
30 Derive
31 Champs Élysées eateries
34 Joy Division lead singer Curtis
37 1960s activist
38 Infield bouncer
39 Act out
44 Racing shells
46 Tickles the fancy
47 Literary foot
50 Served a screamer
51 Great review
52 Fast-talking
53 *An Inconvenient Truth* author
54 Relax
55 *Shark Tale* octopus
56 Get an ___ effort
57 Dirty Harry's org.
59 Persona ___ grata

★★ Sudoku

Fill in the grid so that each row, each column and each 3 x 3 frame contains every number from 1 to 9.

		3	9			8		
		4	5		1	2	9	
3					2	6	5	7
9							2	
		2				9		3
2		8	7	4		3		
				6	8	5	4	
6		5						

SYMBOL SUMS

Can you work out these number sums using three of these four symbols? **+ − ÷ ×**
(No fractions or minus numbers are involved in the sum as you progress from left to right.)

$$7 \square 8 \square 8 \square 16 = 4$$

★ Word Ladder

Convert the word at the top of the ladder into the word at the bottom, using all the rungs in between. On each rung, you must put a valid word that has the same letters as the word above it, apart from one letter change. There may be more than one way of achieving this.

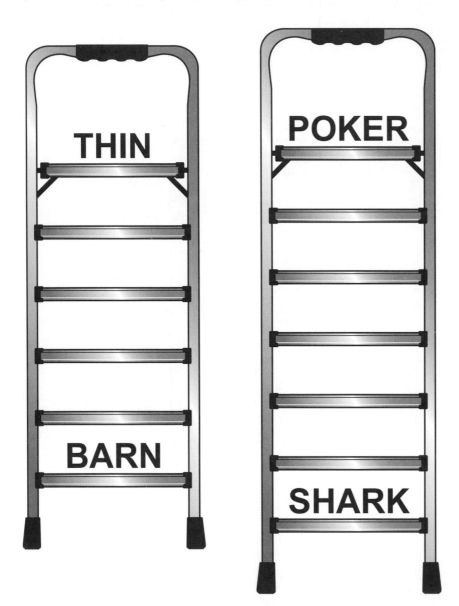

THIN

BARN

POKER

SHARK

FRIENDS?

What do the following words have in common?

MATCH CASH GEAR SHADOW TOOL

★★★ Divine Nature by John M. Samson

ACROSS

1 It means "king" in Persian
5 Snooker shot
10 Plant fiber
14 Surcharge
15 Ease, as anxieties
16 *On the Waterfront* heroine
17 Locality
18 Henry Luce's wife
19 Song finale
20 Popular minivan of 1993–2002
23 "Who am ___ judge?"
24 "___ Take Romance"
25 Inflammation
29 Adds a glossy coating
33 Stage direction
34 Eucharist holder
36 Pluvial
37 Mira Sorvino's Oscar film
41 Laila, the boxer
42 Tattered and torn
43 Hydroxyl compound
44 Sobriquet
46 Trattoria fare
49 Intent
50 "Rubbish!"
51 Mozart opus in C major
60 Voiced
61 Spur attachment
62 Highlands hillside
63 Narrow winning margin
64 Give a lift, in a way
65 Old Testament book
66 Went after legally
67 Checkbook entry
68 Medicos

DOWN

1 Major tennis event
2 Not elsewhere
3 Make a claim
4 Perfume flower
5 Keyboard timesavers
6 Colleague in combat
7 Serb or Croat, for example
8 Calcutta article of clothing
9 Make-up item
10 Make relaxed
11 Sick as ___
12 Fries, e.g.
13 Go like heck
21 Beehive State tribe
22 Range of the southwest
25 Amend an atlas section
26 Deportee
27 "Far out, man!"
28 Cataclysm
29 Grain alcohol
30 *Dallas* clan name
31 Reveal, as a secret
32 Upright pillar
35 On target
38 Blue eyes, for one
39 Talked, talked, talked
40 Scene of some confessions
45 Aced an exam
47 Ornamental band
48 Sample sauce with bread
51 DiMaggio and Louis
52 Pakistani language
53 Signal via beeper
54 Romeo or Juliet
55 Large mop
56 Himalayan haunter
57 Wedding soup pasta
58 Meth lab raider
59 Thumbs-ups

★★★ Futoshiki

Fill in the 5 x 5 grid with the numbers from 1 to 5 once per row and column, while following the greater than/lesser than symbols shown. There is only one valid solution that can be reached through logic and clear thinking alone!

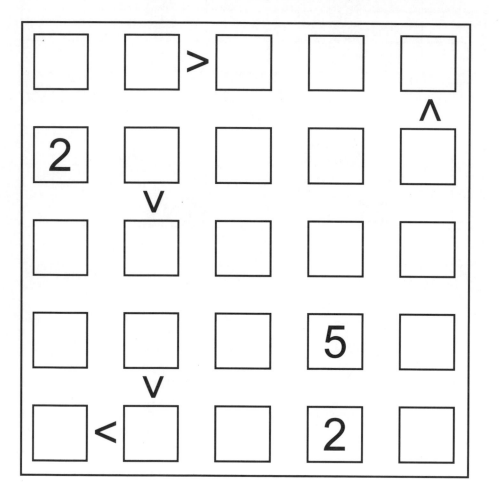

LETTERBLOCKS

Move the letterblocks around so that words are formed on top and below that you can associate with actions. In one block, the letter from the top row has been switched with the letter from the bottom row.

★★ BrainSnack®—Sign of the Times

Which number should replace the question mark?

DOODLE PUZZLE

A doodle puzzle is a combination of images, letters and/or numbers that represent a word or a concept. If you cannot solve a doodle puzzle, do not look at the answer right away. Think hard—and outside the box.

★ Textiles

All the words are hidden vertically, horizontally or diagonally—in both directions. The letters that remain unused form a sentence from left to right.

```
T E X T S W A N S K I N T I L
S S L O O W W E N T C L O T H
N E C M E C E R E M H S A C A
O N Y A S A I D L L T R H A T
T F E I R S N R E T W O E V E
T L S J N L B A T E L U M A U
U E R T E T E N T H W I E T D
B E E E R A I T E R M T U A A
L C J H S K N O R D A E Y Q M
S E I G S N A S R T E T R T A
S T E K N A L B Y F T A T E S
B R C B T I C H C R A T S V K
V U R I A H O M L N P S U L T
B E A K S N H A O E E T D E A
E L L U T A D R T N S E N V M
P I E O A D T A H I T E I I N
S D A D U I F I G L R F E R E
E D A C O R B N N E Y T W A Y
```

INDUSTRY
JEANS
JERSEY
LINEN
MOHAIR
MULETA
NEW WOOL
PLAIT
QUILT
SATIN
SCARLET
SHEET
SILK
STARCH
SUEDE
SWANSKIN
TAPESTRY
TARTAN
TERRY CLOTH
THREAD
TRICOT
TULLE
TWEED
VELOUR
VELVET

BANDAGE
BLANKET
BROCADE

BUCKSKIN
BUTTONS
CASHMERE

CLOTH
DAMASK
FLEECE

DELETE ONE

Delete one letter from SORT BLUES and discover problems.

★★★★ AKA I by Karen Peterson

ACROSS

1 "Hairy man" in Genesis 27:11
5 *Shrek* princess
10 Hoe target
14 Demands payment
15 Cherbourg ciao
16 Garret of *Deadwood*
17 Jerome Silberman aka ___
19 Roil
20 "Flower of my heart" in song
21 Twist
23 Nurse a grudge
24 Chicken feed
25 Go ___ (leave the band)
27 Colorful, crested bird
30 Talk back
33 An Ivy Leaguer
35 *Shark Tale* dragon fish
36 Female turkey
37 In addition
38 "Walk on By" lyricist David
39 Aphrodite's son
41 Gaucho's rope
43 Old dagger
44 Back country
46 Returned to the perch
48 Vanilla beans
49 Sci-fi film set on Pandora
53 Giant tree of California
56 "I, Too, Sing ___": Langston Hughes
57 Particle
58 Richard Starkey aka ___
60 Hardly petite
61 Took a crack at
62 U.S./Canada border lake
63 Aries or Taurus
64 Fool's lack
65 Root beer brand

DOWN

1 Writer Burroughs
2 Glove leather
3 Queen ___ lace
4 Dysfunctional
5 In a whisper
6 Doing nothing
7 Suffix for planet
8 Have to have
9 Outer ear
10 Extravagant one
11 Reginald Dwight aka ___
12 Riyadh royal
13 Blowgun ammo
18 A.A. candidate
22 ___'wester (waterproof hat)
26 Warren in *The Wild Bunch*
27 Flora and fauna
28 Insect wings
29 Where Clinton studied law
30 C&W singer Wooley
31 Houston hockey player
32 Calvin Broadus, Jr. aka ___
34 Mauna ___
40 Snow sculptures
41 Getaways
42 Dessert request
43 Commenced
45 Bachelor's last words
47 Burl in *Summer Magic*
50 Coronation wear
51 Foul-smelling
52 Prime-rib orders
53 Cheering section noises
54 Lady's small case
55 Desperate, as a warning
56 Who-knows-how-long
59 *Collages* novelist Anaïs

★ Spot the Differences

Find the nine differences in the image on the right.

DOUBLETALK

Homophones are words that share the same pronunciation, no matter how they are spelled. If they are spelled differently then they are called heterographs. Find heterographs meaning:

LOCATE and PENALIZED

★ Word Wheel

How many words of three or more letters, each including the letter at the center of the wheel, can you make from this diagram? No plurals or conjugations. We found 22, including one nine-letter word. Can you do better?

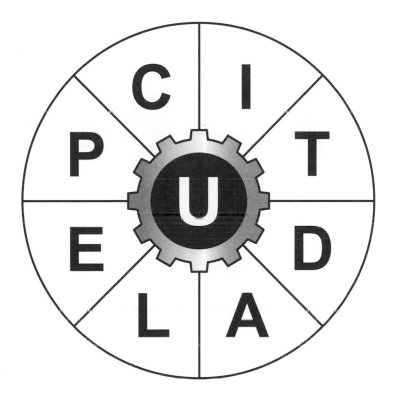

DOODLE PUZZLE

A doodle puzzle is a combination of images, letters and/or numbers that represent a word or a concept. If you cannot solve a doodle puzzle, do not look at the answer right away. Think hard—and outside the box.

★★★★ AKA II by Karen Peterson

ACROSS

1 Heaping Pelion upon ___
5 Toss out
10 Hammer-wielding god
14 *The First Wives* ___ (1996)
15 São ___, Brazil
16 Prefix for graph
17 Anna Mae Bullock aka ___
19 Smudge
20 Praise to the skies
21 Alley X's
23 Exile
24 Justice Ginsburg
25 ___-do-well
27 Understands
30 Put below
33 Pass on, as information
35 "___ in Calico": Crosby
36 Singer Lorain
37 Bud
38 Heavenly altar
39 *Rent* heroine
41 Tricked
43 Tenth Commandment sin
44 Jeff in *True Grit*
46 Laura of the big screen
48 Deal with
49 Nabokov heroine
53 Didn't sink
56 Goes out of business?
57 Hot items
58 Steven Demetre Georgiou aka ___
60 Concerning, in legalese
61 Valuable find
62 German duck
63 Even-steven
64 Footprints
65 Straw home

DOWN

1 Quartet x two
2 Water-park feature
3 Crack of dawn
4 Ornamental shell
5 Speak explosively in anger
6 Solicitude
7 Kennel feature
8 Heady drinks
9 Play on stage
10 *Bewitched* daughter
11 Terry Gene Bollea aka ___
12 Great Plains tribe
13 Becomes compost
18 Allowance for weight
22 Wagon trail
26 Brother of Romulus
27 Went to bat against
28 Fab
29 Vanquish a vampire
30 Suckling sheep
31 Gulf States bigwig
32 Demetria Gene Guynes aka ___
34 Once around at Indy
40 Used one's imagination
41 Uses radar
42 X's out
43 Jazz up
45 Dig, so to speak
47 Unthinking repetition
50 Papas in *Zorba the Greek*
51 Bivouac shelters
52 It's black on the balance sheet
53 Fly like a hummingbird
54 Anderson of *The Mullets*
55 Small pointed missile
56 Send one's regrets
59 Pump part

★★ BrainSnack®—Machine Code

Which letter should replace the question mark?

WORD WALL

Beginning at the left side of the wall, make a
word by adding one group of letters from each
column as you move left to right. When you
have found the first word, go back to the second
column and start the next word, gathering one
group of letters from each column, and so on
until all the letters are used to make six words.

★★ The Puzzled Librarian

The new library assistant accidentally bumped into the Good Reads notice board, and the magnetic letters all fell off. The librarian remembered the authors' names, but needs some help to get the titles right, as the chief librarian will be back in ten minutes!

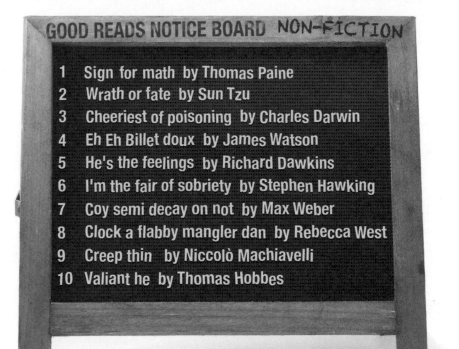

GOOD READS NOTICE BOARD NON-FICTION

1　Sign for math by Thomas Paine
2　Wrath or fate by Sun Tzu
3　Cheeriest of poisoning by Charles Darwin
4　Eh Eh Billet doux by James Watson
5　He's the feelings by Richard Dawkins
6　I'm the fair of sobriety by Stephen Hawking
7　Coy semi decay on not by Max Weber
8　Clock a flabby mangler dan by Rebecca West
9　Creep thin   by Niccolò Machiavelli
10　Valiant he by Thomas Hobbes

DOODLE PUZZLE

A doodle puzzle is a combination of images, letters and/or numbers that represent a word or a concept. If you cannot solve a doodle puzzle, do not look at the answer right away. Think hard—and outside the box.

★★★★ Before and After by John M. Samson

ACROSS

1 *There's Something About ___* (1998)
5 *Beauty and the Beast* teapot
10 "I almost forgot ..."
14 Away from the wind, on a yacht
15 "Sail on, ___ of State!": Longfellow
16 Utensil
17 Game show gal/First Family home
20 Finalize
21 Border collie
22 Powerful person
24 Childcare writer LeShan
25 Horse of a certain color
28 Alien ships
30 Splinter
35 Rainbow goddess
37 A few, to Francisco
39 *Absolutely Fabulous* role
40 Tenacious D member/ Thanksgiving follower
43 Ninja Turtles cohort April
44 Deanna of *Star Trek: TNG*
45 Córdoban cat
46 Shark on the links
48 Bern river
50 *Funeral in Berlin* author Deighton
51 Put-down, in the hood
53 Meadows
55 Hypothetical
60 Strive toward an end
64 "Godfather of Soul"/ freshwater fish
66 Parroted
67 Paul in *Stateside*
68 2012 UFC champion José
69 Actor Auberjonois
70 Paradises
71 Harry Potter, for one

DOWN

1 Dallas hoopsters
2 Wings, in old Rome
3 "Will I?" Broadway musical
4 1983 Streisand film
5 Mighty
6 Kyrgyzstan city
7 "___ Boy": Beatles
8 Church pledge
9 Passes a limit
10 Seated on
11 Vibrant
12 Not good, but not bad
13 Mr. Cassini
18 Baseball brothers
19 Medicine man
23 *The 39 Steps* star
25 Mustard with a kick
26 Heavens: Comb. form
27 Sweeter
29 Pelvic bones
31 Beatnik's "Got it!"
32 *1876* author
33 Mother's kin
34 Textile type
36 Read cursorily
38 "To your health!"
41 Schick Quattro foursome
42 Stinging insects
47 "Jack Be ___"
49 90 degrees from north
52 Begot
54 Herringlike fish
55 Cracked, as a door
56 Dracula's wear
57 Grace ender
58 "___ Dinah": Frankie Avalon
59 Johnny-___-lately
61 Captive of Hercules
62 Unmannered
63 Thames River town
65 White as a ghost

★★★ Binairo

Complete the grid with zeros and ones until there are 6 zeros and 6 ones in every row and every column. No more than two of the same number can be next to or under each other. Rows or columns with exactly the same content are not allowed. There is only one valid solution.

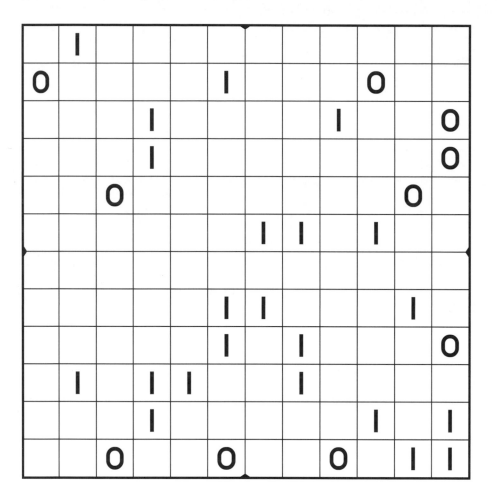

SYMBOL SUMS

Can you work out these number sums using three of these four symbols? ＋ − ÷ ✕
(No fractions or minus numbers are involved in the sum as you progress from left to right.)

$$21 \ \square \ 8 \ \square \ 6 \ \square \ 2 = 39$$

★★ Keep Going

Start on a blank square of your choice and connect as many blank squares as possible with one single continuous line. You can only connect squares along vertical and horizontal lines. You must continue the connecting line up until the next obstacle, i.e., the rim of the box, a black square or a square that has already been used. You can change direction at any obstacle you meet. Each square can be used only once. The number of blank squares that will be left unused is marked in the upper square. There is more than one solution. We show only one solution.

FRIENDS?

What do the following words have in common?

CRYSTAL CLOTHES BORDER BLOOD COAST

★★★★ In the Vanguard by Linda Lather

ACROSS
1 Irish Spring, e.g.
5 Ignorance, to some
10 Send headlong
14 Word with happy or zero
15 Show of a scarce vowel
16 Cross a stream, say
17 Poet Pound
18 Cost ___ and a leg
19 Self-cleaning appliance
20 Certain cross-examination query
23 Like some lots and socks
24 1052, in a proclamation
25 *Monty Python's Flying Circus* producer
28 Go nuts
31 Mountaineer Hillary
35 Diamond Head locale
37 Austrian artist Schiele
39 Selection word
40 Feature of many autos
43 Hatchet man
44 Outermost of the Aleutian Islands
45 Goblet feature
46 Affording beautiful vistas
48 Jets with delta wings
50 Doubles in tennis?
51 Big ball
53 "A likely story!"
55 On the cutting edge
63 Fearsome tooth
64 Suitor
65 Assembly of competitors
66 Novel ending
67 Water wheel
68 "Do ___ others ..."
69 Another man's flower
70 Rudder's spot
71 Not long

DOWN
1 "Spaghetti" poet Silverstein
2 Move viscously
3 Enveloping atmosphere
4 Home of many Goyas
5 Just released
6 Country singer k.d.
7 Desert Storm arena
8 Syringe filler
9 Mother of Bacchus
10 Double-crossers
11 Saxophonist Coltrane
12 Thought: Comb. form
13 Sean in *Mystic River*
21 Passports et al.
22 Agreed (with)
25 Broadway hits, in slang

26 Containing element #56
27 Dusting, e.g.
29 Turkish lord
30 *Dead ___ Society* (1989)
32 Come together
33 David in *The Pink Panther*
34 Has an opinion
36 Not promised to
38 New Jersey cagers
41 Three-toned chord
42 Protestant sect
47 Rodeo distractions
49 Cul-de-___
52 Going on, to Sherlock
54 Organic soil material
55 Half a dozen, say
56 Despise

57 Grafted, in heraldry
58 Went like the wind
59 Next in line
60 Neighbor of Sparks, Nevada
61 Nix from the governor
62 Hugh Laurie's alma mater

★★★ Sport Maze

Draw the shortest way from the ball to the goal. You can only move along vertical and horizontal lines, not along diagonal lines. The figure on each square indicates the number of squares the ball must be moved in the same direction. You can change direction at each stop.

4	3	4	5	5	4
0	0	1	1	1	1
(1)	1	1	0	0	0
3	3	3	3	4	5
3	1	1	1	4	●
1	4	1	5	5	3

ONE LETTER LESS OR MORE

The word on the right side contains the letters of the word on the left side plus or minus the letter in the middle. One letter is already in the right place.

L A C R O S S E +E ☐ ☐ ☐ S ☐ ☐ ☐ ☐

★★ BrainSnack®—Finger

When investigating this fingerprint the detective relies mainly on the red dots. Which dot (1–6) is in the wrong position?

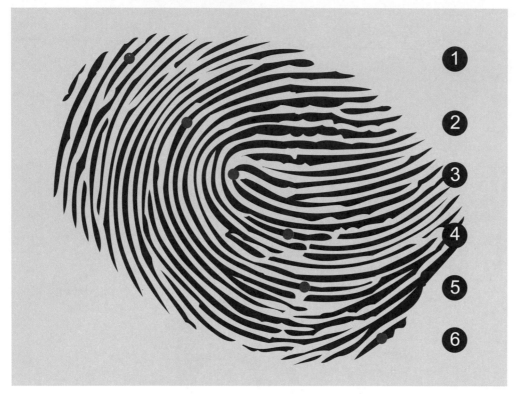

BLOCK ANAGRAM

Form the word that is described in the brackets with the letters above the grid. Extra letters are already in the right place.

PHOTOGIRL (studies handwriting)

★★★★ Night Lights by Karen Peterson

ACROSS

1 ___ *Male War Bride* (1949)
6 Prudent, as advice
10 Mrs. Garrett on *The Facts of Life*
14 Libyan coin
15 Outback birds
16 Place to park it
17 Tedium
18 Green Chevrolet
19 ___-nine-tails
20 1988 Richard Dreyfuss film
23 G ___ "George"
24 Convertiplane, in brief
25 Shar-___ dog
28 Eight: Comb. form
30 Chalk remover
34 Lanchester in *The Bishop's Wife*
36 Ethereal prefix
38 Keyboard piece
39 2002 sci-fi film
42 Rockne was one
43 *The Concrete Jungle* actress Talbot
44 Aarhus resident
45 Many rulers have 12
47 Kind of egg
49 Cole of song
50 "Flying Scotsman" Liddell
52 Where some sheep sleep
54 Downtown Disney theme restaurant
61 Splash Mountain, e.g.
62 Dice unit
63 Specialized talk
64 Biblical evictee
65 Of the ear
66 Iridescent stones
67 One of two English queens
68 Come together
69 Zellweger in *Miss Potter*

DOWN

1 As above, in footnotes
2 Lush
3 ___ Domini
4 Site to sweat it out
5 Musical passage
6 Booth Tarkington book
7 Youngest god
8 Chug-a-lugs
9 Many-acred residence
10 Stepped up
11 Rock's Grateful ___
12 Pact since WW2
13 Suffix for fabric
21 Chapel cleric
22 *Sky Music* composer
25 Joe in *The Good Shepherd*
26 "Your Song" singer John
27 Child taken to Moriah as a sacrifice
29 *The In-Laws* actor Alan
31 Gordon's wife on *Sesame Street*
32 *Absolutely Fabulous* character
33 Fix the blinking 12:00
35 Lex Luthor, to Superman
37 Mind
40 First word of many limericks
41 Studio prop
46 *The Office* is one
48 President for 16 months
51 Rodeo holding pen
53 Pick pockets
54 Victoria Park stroller
55 Rose in a *Music Man* song
56 Feast of Esther month
57 Theater award since 1956
58 *Faithful* coauthor Stewart
59 Gaze amorously
60 Medicine bottle notation

★ Roman Empire

All the words are hidden vertically, horizontally or diagonally—in both directions. The letters that remain unused form a sentence from left to right.

```
L T H E R O A S M E A N I K S
Z E N O E I U M M P E I I B R
E P G R V I O P B G A N E A D
L B L I D Y I B A E G L P I I
C U L U O R T H A D P M M T C
E T A O E N T E O S O L O E T
A L R G G R S M U E E T P R A
C N F R A N K S O T B E E C T
B H O C O N S U L A O B E U O
P A O C R O A P E R I N E L R
V N R R I C L T H T E Y S G O
E N E B I B A V O S L A V E S
S I N R A N U P R I N C E P S
U B F E E R R A G R I P P A
V A N S E E I D C A E S A R A
I L N D P M R A E M O T E C T
U R E D R U M E N S U T U R B
S U T I T S D H I S P A N I A
```

EMPIRE
FRANKS
GAUL
HANNIBAL
HISPANIA
HORACE
KINGDOM
LEGIONS
LIVIA
LUCRETIA
MAGISTRATES
MURDER
NERO
PLEBS
POMPEII
PRINCEPS
REMUS
RUBICON
SENATE
SENECA
SLAVES
TEUTONS
TIBER
TITUS
VESUVIUS
ZENO

AFRICA
AGRIPPA
BARBARIANS

BRUTUS
CAESAR
CARTHAGE

CLAUDIUS
CONSUL
DICTATOR

DELETE ONE

Delete one letter from HOSPITAL TOGAS and find someone who might wear one.

★★ Word Sudoku

Complete the grid so that each row, each column and each 3 x 3 frame contains the nine letters from the black box below. The hidden nine-letter word is in the diagonal from top left to bottom right.

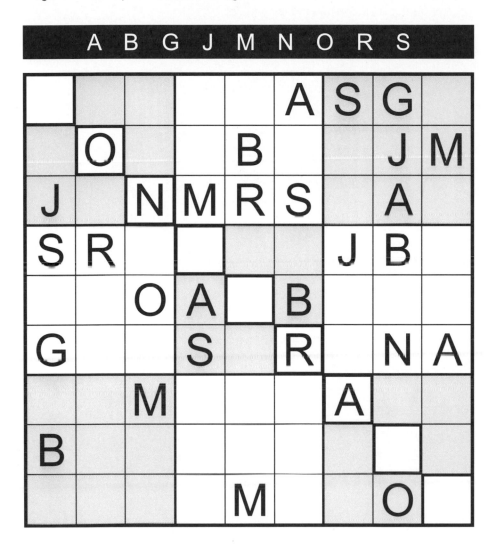

A B G J M N O R S

UNCANNY TURN

Rearrange the letters of the phrase below to form a cognate anagram, one which is related or connected in meaning to the original phrase. The answer can be one or more words.

SHADOW REFLECTS DOOM

★★ Sunny Weather

Where will the sun shine? With the knowledge that each arrow points to a place where a symbol should be, can you locate the sunny spots? The symbols cannot be next to each other vertically, horizontally or diagonally. A symbol cannot be placed on top of an arrow. We show one symbol.

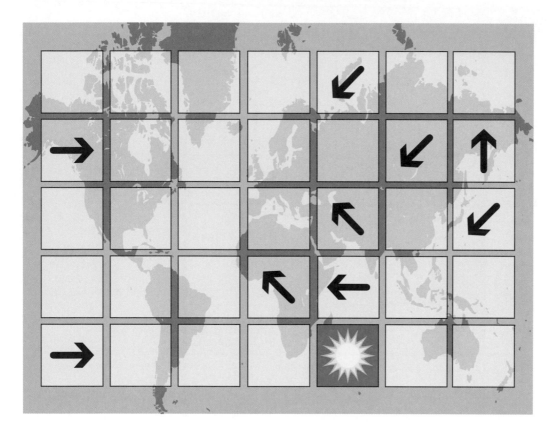

TRIANAGRAM

Three-word groups of anagrams are also called triplets or trianagrams.
Complete the group:

CATERED   _ _ _ _ _ _ _   _ _ _ _ _ _ _

★★★★ Stripes by John M. Samson

ACROSS

1 Magician's hiding spot
5 Outspoken
10 Girder of a sort
14 Notion
15 Polynesian greeting
16 Many an opening event
17 Treats with stripes
19 Magnitogorsk river
20 Crafty one?
21 Ghastly
23 Come into
24 "Long Time ___": Dixie Chicks
25 Garb
29 "Get ready!"
32 Alpine pool
33 Feel without touching
35 Floored it
36 Pasta suffix
37 Bird in a cage, e.g.
38 Japan's largest lake
39 Henley's *The ___ Firecracker Contest*
41 Confuse
43 Nations in solidarity
44 Two-wheeled vehicle
46 Worst off
48 First capital of Japan
49 He opened the 1996 Olympics
50 Agape
53 They may be busts
57 Not yet risen
58 Ways with stripes
60 Small estuaries
61 High roost
62 "The proof ___ the pudding"
63 Adopted son of Claudius
64 Southern side dish
65 Wash. ball club

DOWN

1 About 1/6 inch
2 Nisan's antecedent
3 Good Friday's time
4 Amy in *Field of Dreams*
5 Moves out
6 *The Good Earth* heroine
7 Cheat
8 Cousin of "psst!"
9 Baked Italian dish
10 Spiny lizards
11 Sign with stripes
12 Apple spray of yore
13 Unhealthy rattle
18 Flanders river
22 Slip a ___ (err)
25 Molecule makeup
26 Lose one's cool
27 Clothes with stripes
28 Social outcast
29 Thwart in court
30 Aspiring singer's tapes
31 It's the law
34 Ship-shaped clock
40 Scoundrel
41 Legless chair
42 Graffiti beards
43 Largest European island
45 Glyceride lead-in
47 One of five Norwegian kings
50 Adventurer's tale
51 Anne Nichols hero
52 Opera or concert attachment
53 Like some skirts
54 Bear in the heavens
55 Cut film
56 Form data: Abbr.
59 Mystifier Geller

★ Horoscope

Fill in the grid so that every row, every column and every frame of six boxes contains six different symbols: health, work, money, happiness, family and love. Look at the row or column that corresponds with your sign of the zodiac and find out which of the six symbols are important for you today. The symbols appear in increasing order of importance (1–6). It's up to you to translate the meaning of each symbol to your specific situation.

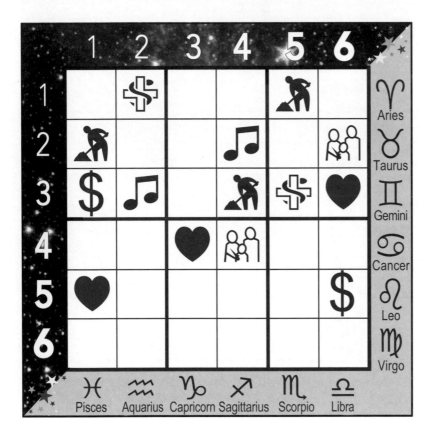

WORD WALL

Beginning at the left side of the wall, make a word by adding one group of letters from each column as you move left to right. When you have found the first word, go back to the second column and start the next word, gathering one group of letters from each column, and so on until all the letters are used to make six words.

★★ BrainSnack®—Pad Puzzle

How many items are in the TV tube folder?

LETTERBLOCKS

Move the letterblocks around so that words are formed on top and below that you can associate with fabrics.

★★★★ Tennis Talk by Michele Sayer

ACROSS
1 Mideast bigwig
5 Hydra, e.g.
10 Verve
14 Oasis fruit
15 Keep ___ to the ground
16 AOL triangle, e.g.
17 Jim Carrey title role
19 "___ so sorry"
20 Reminder
21 Make out
23 Classic Japanese drama
24 Caterpillar hair
25 Curly lock
29 Afraid
32 Plaintiff
33 Got hitched again
35 Jimi Hendrix hairstyle
36 Singer "King" Cole
37 *Batman* sound effect
38 Back in time
39 Spaces between
41 Like winter coats
43 Dessert choices
44 Exploited, slangily
46 Compunction
48 Olive in a Caesar salad?
49 Gazetteer feature
50 Has another opinion
53 Sets fire to
57 Et ___ (and others)
58 Venue for a moonlighting judge?
60 Keep them about you
61 Follow immediately
62 Nashville star McEntire
63 "Candy is dandy ..." poet
64 Absorbs books
65 Muscovite's refusal

DOWN
1 Round Dutch cheese
2 Nutmeg spice
3 Inventory unit
4 Crime motive
5 Mountain lion
6 Knowing about
7 Bucharest coin
8 Badminton spot
9 Gave a big hand to
10 Cathy's cartoon dog
11 Amour
12 Stress may be one
13 Norse goddess of fate
18 Chemical compound
22 Locale of Davy Jones' locker
25 Ladder steps

26 Violinist Stern
27 Earnings
28 At room temperature
29 Reduced in number
30 Presses
31 Baggy
34 Emerged victorious
40 Egocentric
41 Novitiate
42 Removes stripes
43 Movie munchie
45 Minute
47 Muralist Chagall
50 First light
51 Gold-medalist skater Kulik
52 Trig function
53 Dull noise

54 Donald Duck's nephew
55 Kathryn of *Law & Order: CI*
56 On the double!
59 U.S procurement agcy.

★★★ Sudoku

Fill in the grid so that each row, each column and each 3 x 3 frame contains every number from 1 to 9.

2	4		9		8		7	
	5	8		6				
		9		5			2	8
		1				7		
			6		3	4		9
			4				1	
5					9			
	6		1	8				
		7						

SYMBOL SUMS

Can you work out these number sums using three of these four symbols? **＋ － ÷ ✕**
(No fractions or minus numbers are involved in the sum as you progress from left to right.)

$$6 \,\square\, 4 \,\square\, 4 \,\square\, 4 = 5$$

★★ Number Cluster

Complete the grid by constituting adjoining clusters that consist of as many
cubes as the number on the cubes. At cube 5, for instance, you will have to make
a five-cube cluster. Two or more figure cubes of the same value belong to the
same cluster. You can only place your cubes along horizontal and/or vertical lines.

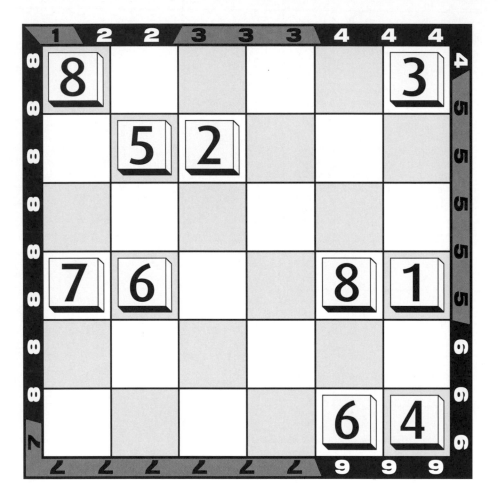

SANDWICH

What five-letter word belongs between the word on the left and the word on the right, so that
the first and second word, and the second and third word, each form a common compound word
or phrase?

HOBBY _ _ _ _ _ HAIR

★★★★ Riders by Peggy O'Shea

ACROSS

1 Tiebreaker result
5 Where Hawthorne wrote *The Scarlet Letter*
10 1944 ETO battleground
14 Where Bountiful is
15 Mariner's friend in *Waterworld*
16 "If ___ a Hammer"
17 Silver's rider
19 Aloha State bird
20 Serving no purpose
21 Flies the coop
23 502, in Roman numerals
24 "Thirty days ___ September ..."
25 Nougat nuts
29 Do the voice-over
32 Borrowed (with "on")
33 Support for an artist
35 Blue dye source
36 I topper
37 Marty McFly's friend
38 Jazz guitarist Farlow
39 Small newts
41 Torpedoes
43 Ripped
44 Project glowingly
46 P.T. Barnum, notably
48 *Young Frankenstein* girl
49 Yale alum
50 McDowell in *Halloween II*
53 Last Supper figure
57 Code word for "A"
58 Llamrei's rider
60 Robin Hood's beneficiaries
61 Eastern VIP
62 Grown-up elvers
63 "Auld Lang ___"
64 Marry again
65 It's played on a stage

DOWN

1 Humdinger
2 Platte River tribe
3 Playing with a full deck
4 Misery befell him in *Misery*
5 Oceanfront
6 Landers and Miller
7 Ship captain's account
8 Robert on Traveller
9 27 Down, for one
10 Frank in *High Society*
11 Hero's rider
12 Country path
13 Poems that were sung originally
18 Bridle attachment
22 Nissan Leaf, for one
25 Waterproof wood
26 Shower sponge
27 Buck's rider
28 "Sexy" girl in a Beatles song
29 Narrow parts
30 Pope's crown
31 Page in *Juno*
34 Father's Day giver
40 Not false
41 Star's nightmare
42 First American in space
43 Storm chaser's target
45 "Long, long ___ ..."
47 Genus of swans
50 Results of genetic research
51 "If I Were ___": Beyoncé
52 Charades performer
53 "Miracle Mets" outfielder
54 Vincent van Gogh's brother
55 Respite
56 Celtic language
59 Innovative

★★ Concentration—Only One

Try to draw this shape with one continuous line without lifting your pencil off the page and without any overlapping.

DOODLE PUZZLE

A doodle puzzle is a combination of images, letters and/or numbers that represent a word or a concept. If you cannot solve a doodle puzzle, do not look at the answer right away. Think hard—and outside the box.

★★ BrainSnack®—Route Finder

Where (A–I) will the GPS have the driver leave the map?

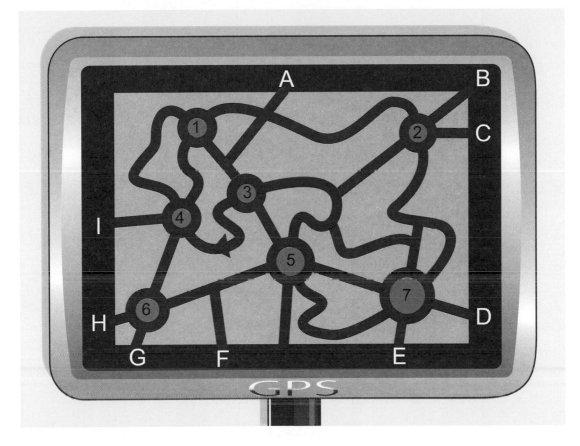

CHANGELINGS

Each of the three lines of letters below spell names of occupations, but the letters have been mixed up. Four letters from the first word are now in the third line, four letters from the third word are in the second line and four letters from the second word are in the first line. The remaining letters are in their original places. What are the words?

J A S T R L C S O R
D O U R N E M I K T
I R N S S U A T E R

★★★★ On the Strip by John M. Samson

ACROSS

1 ___ metabolism
6 European high points
10 Silicate used as an insulator
14 Plato's marketplace
15 Jim Nabors' soldier role
16 Yankee slugger
17 Perfumed powders
18 Blueprint
19 Songsmith Porter
20 Robert Louis Stevenson novel*
23 Lady of Spain
24 Honeybunch
25 "___ Talkin' ": Bee Gees
28 ATM need
30 Victorian, in a way
34 "Harvest" singer DiFranco
35 Painted Desert sights
37 Acclimatize
38 What answers to clues* are
41 Paid for a hand
42 Tamarack
43 Eight-ball stick
44 Units of wisdom?
46 Jacobi in *Avalon*
47 Many adoptees
48 Puppy plaint
50 Sevier Lake locale
52 Yankee Stadium song*
58 Slow story
59 Musical disk
60 Pond greenery
61 Black-hearted
62 Succulent herb
63 First two-time Nobelist
64 Rolex face
65 New Jersey players
66 Success has a sweet one

DOWN

1 Cotton sheet
2 Food thickener
3 Loafer part
4 *Mortal Kombat* milieu
5 Calf roper's handful
6 Evaluation
7 Grammy winner Lovett
8 *Dead Men Don't Wear ___* (1982)
9 Has a gut feeling
10 Yankee Doodle's "feather"
11 Item in Tiger's bag
12 Frosty
13 Citrus drink
21 Let float, as a currency
22 Running a bit behind schedule
25 Mexican cathartic
26 Ludicrous
27 Windows 7 predecessor
29 Like SpongeBob's voice
31 Corner chair occupant
32 Tiler's mortar
33 Concurrences
35 Musical mixture
36 Mooches
39 "All right then ..."
40 Less than right?
45 Party catchphrase
47 Taxonomic division
49 Common worker
51 Flying radar station
52 *Avatar* aliens
53 "Grace Before Meat" essayist
54 Clove hitch, e.g.
55 Fiend of dreams
56 Bannister
57 Howard of *Annie Get Your Gun*
58 Guitarist Nugent

★ Volcanos

All the words are hidden vertically, horizontally or diagonally—in both directions. The letters that remain unused form a sentence from left to right.

```
T K H E E V E S U V I U S R D
I A C T I V E U P T J I O I A
I M N O F A S E U P U E O A C
E C R E C R U S T V F R M D I
P H E O X L C A N N I G U G T
M A O L H T A E D T A O E E E
O T G C A A I N E M L Y A O T
P K G R W N L N D C S N H L L
A A A V A E D A G E C A T O A
A R B S I N E N R U S T R G S
A O B P I L I H O M I I I Y A
C C R C T W O T N I S S T E B
I Q O N O U E N E C S E H E S
R A A L T N A M R O D S N E D
E M G L E T A A D L E F I E D
M E V I S O L P X E T O A M N
A E W I C B N I A T N U O M E
E A G C R A T E R J E L A V A
```

EXPLOSIVE
EXTINGUISHED
FUJI
GABBRO
GEOLOGY
GEYSER
GLOWING CLOUD
GRANITE
HAWAII
ICELAND
JAPAN
KAMCHATKA
LAVA
MAGMA
MANTLE
MOUNTAIN
POMPEII
TOBA
VESUVIUS

ACTIVE	BASALT	DIORITE
ALARM	CRATER	DORMANT
AMERICA	CRUST	EIFEL
ANDESITE	DACITE	EMISSION
ARARAT	DEATH	ETNA

DELETE ONE

Delete one letter from INCA MATERIALS and find where you might discover them.

★★★ Sudoku X

Fill in the grid so that each row, each column and each 3 x 3 frame contains every number from 1 to 9. The two main diagonals of the grid also contain every number from 1 to 9.

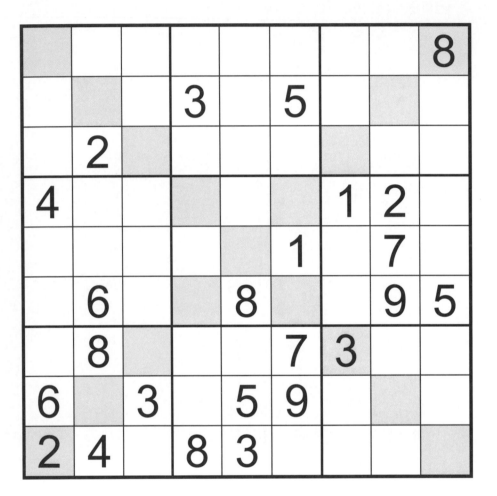

BLOCK ANAGRAM

Form the word that is described in the brackets with the letters above the grid. Extra letters are already in the right place.

HOROLOGIST (bird watcher)

★★★★ Close Encounters by Maggie Ellis

ACROSS

1 Uproar
6 Two-masted sailboat
10 Pintail duck
14 Division signs
15 Potpourri
16 To ___ his own
17 Green finch
18 Tick off
19 Title for a big Turk
20 Comedian encounters film director
23 Punk rock genre
24 Twitch
25 Soundtrack insertion
28 Expectant
31 Stunned and speechless
35 2011 Jay-Z/Kanye West song
37 Lacquered metalware
39 Prefix for "sun"
40 Golfer encounters business baron
43 ___ de menthe
44 Carlisle's wife in *Twilight*
45 Blackthorn fruit
46 Blanched salad green
48 Stereo preceder
50 +
51 French denial
52 Suffix for expert
54 Rock star encounters U.S. senator
63 Christmas carol
64 Award for David Mamet
65 Wanted-poster word
66 Intro to mi
67 Skywalker's teacher
68 O'Reilly of *M*A*S*H*
69 Cross-country gear
70 Blind a falcon
71 Dictation whiz

DOWN

1 *Bonanza* brother
2 Assist a prankster
3 *Billy Budd* captain
4 EVOO part
5 Stanley Kubrick's art
6 Meditative discipline
7 Banned pesticide
8 Chamberlain of basketball fame
9 Davidovich in *Hollywood Homicide*
10 "Needles and Pins" group
11 Crèche trio
12 German for "genuine"
13 Question start
21 Slogan
22 Kind of court
25 La ___ Vita (1960)
26 Road reversal
27 Took the Schwinn
29 Actress Skye
30 Milk whey
32 "Be-Bop-___" (1956 hit)
33 Cowell of *The X Factor*
34 Imbibed
36 Florida State team
38 *Sesame Street* Muppet
41 English cattle breed
42 Material for Strauss
47 Cherishes
49 Awards for *The Artist*
53 Standing ovation, e.g.
54 Wide receivers
55 U.S. magazine (1937–71)
56 *Burnt Toast* author Hatcher
57 Instrument of African blackwood
58 Cloak
59 Boortz of talk radio
60 Mayor's underling
61 John, in Moscow
62 *Quo Vadis?* emperor

★★ Keep Going

Start on a blank square of your choice and connect as many blank squares as possible with one single continuous line. You can only connect squares along vertical and horizontal lines. You must continue the connecting line up until the next obstacle, i.e., the rim of the box, a black square or a square that has already been used. You can change direction at any obstacle you meet. Each square can be used only once. The number of blank squares that will be left unused is marked in the upper square. There is more than one solution. We show only one solution.

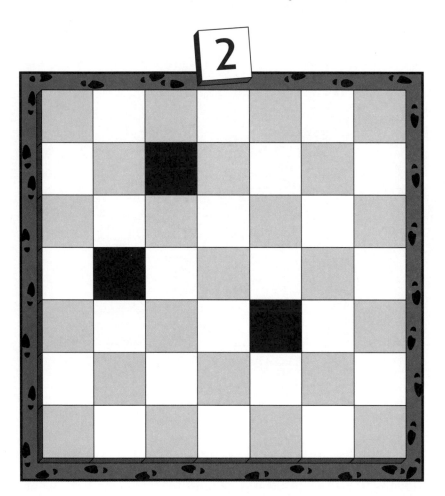

FRIENDS?

What do the following words have in common?

AFTER CATCH CROSS PASS WATCH HEAD

★★★ Sport Maze

Draw the shortest way from the ball to the goal. You can only move along vertical and horizontal lines, not along diagonal lines. The figure on each square indicates the number of squares the ball must be moved in the same direction. You can change direction at each stop.

5	3	5	5	1	4
5	4	4	3	3	5
2	4	1	1	0	4
5	1	2	2	4	5
1	2	1	3	1	5
2	2	5	4	1	

ONE LETTER LESS OR MORE

The word on the right side contains the letters of the word on the left side plus or minus the letter in the middle. One letter is already in the right place.

N E S T L I N G +I ☐ ☐ S ☐ ☐ ☐ ☐ ☐

★★ **BrainSnack®—City Lights**

How many lights should be burning in skyscraper 5?

LETTER LINE

Put a letter in each of the squares below to make a word which is a body of literate consumers. The number clues refer to other words which can be made from the whole.

3 4 8 2 1 2 STICK; 7 8 2 3 1 2 4 CLIPPED;
7 10 1 2 3 4 2 1 DEVICE FOR SCATTERING;
7 8 3 1 2 4 DIVIDED WITH OTHERS; 6 9 10 2 READY

1	2	3	4	5	6	7	8	9	10

★★★★★ Movie Quotes I by Mary Leonard

ACROSS

1 King David's predecessor
5 Pelota basket
10 Bambi, as an adult
14 In addition
15 *You Can't Go Home* ___: Wolfe
16 Wallenda family patriarch
17 "Here's looking at you, kid." film
19 Auto bar
20 Topography
21 Convention address
23 ___ *for Noose*: Grafton
24 Acceptability, for short
25 Orchid color
29 Like some steaks
32 Genus of trumpeter swans
33 Analyze ore
35 Web spot
36 Tim Tebow's org.
37 Undermine
38 Maria ___ Trapp
39 "Another Pyramid" musical
41 Monogrammed, in a way
43 One penny's worth
44 Kaput
46 Change directions
48 Elbe tributary
49 Stiller in *Dodgeball*
50 Calmed down
53 "___ in the Air": Don McLean
57 Persuade
58 "Greed, for lack of a better word, is good." film
60 Young or old ending
61 Come afterward
62 Pearl Mosque site
63 Word said while raising a hand
64 Fawned over
65 Bird with a crazy laugh

DOWN

1 Subgroup
2 Mosquito wings
3 Khrushchev's concern
4 Apprentice
5 Actress Flockhart
6 Alaska's first governor
7 ___ Francisco
8 *Dora the Explorer* squirrel
9 Complete disorder
10 Rollerbladers
11 "You talkin' to me?" film
12 Folk singer Guthrie
13 Singer Campbell
18 Barbara of *Mission: Impossible*
22 Twinkling altar
25 Amoeba, for one
26 "Make a married woman laugh and you're halfway there." film
27 "My name is Pussy Galore." film
28 Resource
29 Bank job, e.g.
30 Berkshire jackets
31 Al ___ (pasta request)
34 Toothy tool
40 No-frills
41 Attached, in a way
42 Lowered in value
43 Midway
45 "___ Blu Dipinto di Blu"
47 Life jacket, for one
50 Be effusive
51 Art Deco artist
52 Paul in *Little Miss Sunshine*
53 Fingerprint, say
54 Plastic block
55 The younger Saarinen
56 Laurel in *The Music Box*
59 *The Longest Day* ship

★★★ Word Sudoku

Complete the grid so that each row, each column and each 3 x 3 frame contains the nine letters from the black box below. The hidden nine-letter word is in the diagonal from top left to bottom right.

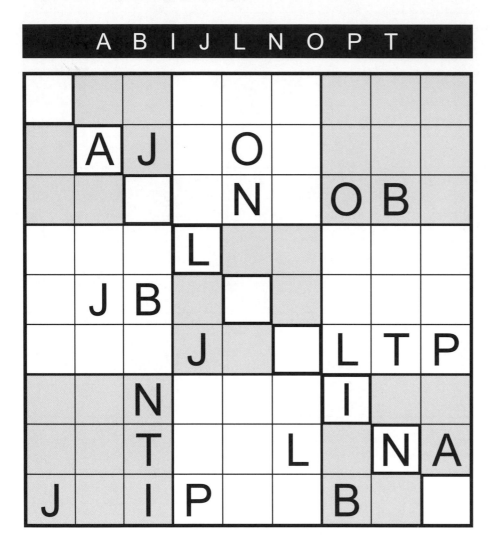

A B I J L N O P T

UNCANNY TURN

Rearrange the letters of the phrase below to form a cognate anagram, one which is related or connected in meaning to the original phrase. The answer can be one or more words.

A WINTER BIAS HERE

★★★ Kakuro

Each number in a black area is the sum of the numbers that you have to enter in the next empty boxes. The empty boxes that make up the sum are called a run. The sum of the across run is written above the diagonal in the black area and the sum of the down run is written below the diagonal. Runs can only contain the numbers 1 through 9 and each number in a run can only be used once. The gray boxes only contain odd numbers and the white only even numbers.

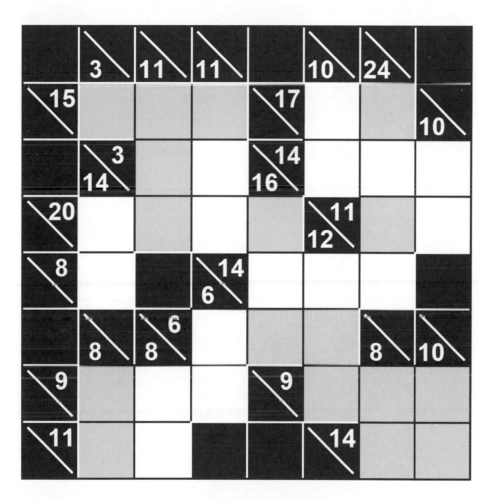

DOUBLETALK

Homophones are words that share the same pronunciation, no matter how they are spelled. If they are spelled differently then they are called heterographs. Find heterographs meaning:

BREACHED and GRIP

★★★★★ Movie Quotes II by Mary Leonard

ACROSS

1 Drop anchor
5 Moisten overnight
10 "Regrets, I've had ___ ..."
14 Texas Hold'em stake
15 Ship out
16 Additional
17 "Being a gangster was better than being president ..." film
19 Party cheese
20 Serpentine sound
21 Mixed a drink
23 Soda bottle units
26 Bacchanal cry
27 Humiliated
29 Bedroom fixture
32 Scott of an 1857 Supreme Court case
33 *The Odd Couple* playwright
35 Mount whose name means "I burn"
36 Straggle
37 Word with horn or filter
38 School of whales
39 Spooky
41 Retinue
43 Not too bright
44 The 13th Amendment abolished it
46 Sweet apple coating
48 ___, mi, fa, sol ...
49 Taste
50 Horrific wave
53 *Hamlet* has five
54 Oomph
55 "Every man dies, not every man really lives." film
60 Parker in *Red Tails*
61 Loch NNE of Edinburgh
62 Timber wolf
63 Uses indigo
64 Sovereign proclamation
65 Willowy

DOWN

1 Wheel type
2 Sushi master Jiro
3 Ear: prefix
4 Carrot-top
5 Sanctifies
6 Congers
7 East Indian lentil dish
8 Spacewalks, for short
9 Horse opera
10 Lauren of *Six Feet Under*
11 "Stupid is as stupid does." film
12 A Great Lake
13 Wild carrot, e.g.
18 Not shaky
22 "___ got it!"
23 Dips out
24 Galilee locale
25 "Plastics." film
28 Pepys' claim to fame
29 Like some Greek columns
30 Porcelain glaze
31 Digress
34 Farrow in *The Great Gatsby*
40 De Carlo and Mitchell
41 Show fear, in a way
42 Just emerging
43 Camelot lasses
45 Big Band ___
47 "Jabberwocky" creature
50 Look after
51 Do in
52 Seething
53 With, in Paris
56 Marvel Studios founder Arad
57 *The Huffington Post* parent
58 Stat for a Yankee
59 Singer Petty

★★★ Sudoku Twin

Fill in the grid so that each row, each column and each 3 x 3 frame contains every number from 1 to 9. A sudoku twin is two connected 9 x 9 sudokus.

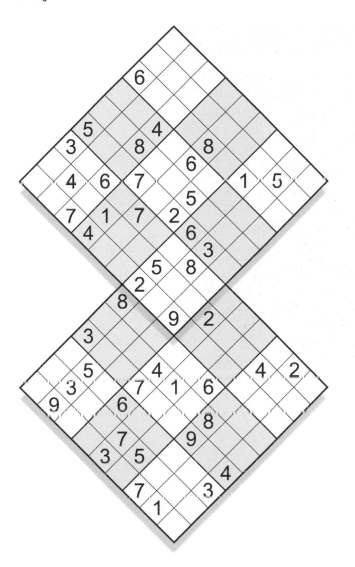

TRIANAGRAM

Three-word groups of anagrams are also called triplets or trianagrams.
Complete the group:

E A R N E S T _ _ _ _ _ _ _   _ _ _ _ _ _ _

★★★ BrainSnack®—Love All

Give the coordinates of the location where the tennis ball will hit the net.
Answer like this: 4D.

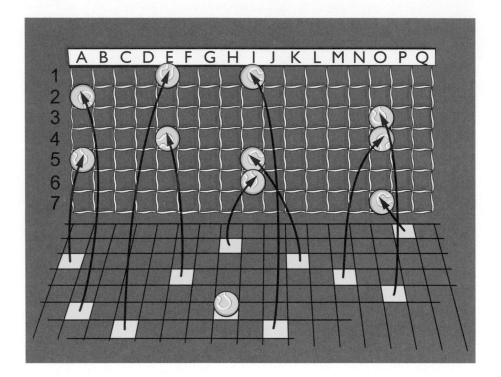

QUICK CROSSWORD

Place the words associated with sports listed below in the crossword grid.

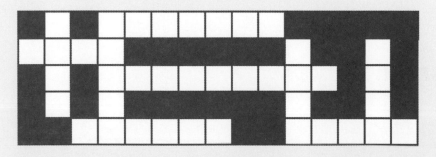

DECATHLON RAFTING YOGA RODEO GOLF POOL POLO ROWING FIELD

★★★★★ **Uniform Numbers** by Michele Sayer

ACROSS

1 "Terrif!"
5 Orinoco River source
10 Battle site in Normandy
14 Invention starter
15 Flora and fauna of a region
16 In trouble, in the Army
17 Snitched on
18 "Shoo!"
19 Neuwirth or Daniels
20 Number worn by A-Rod
22 Purple dinosaur
24 Palmer, to pals
25 The U of BTU
26 Links up
31 *Grand ___ Suite*: Grofé
34 Got off one's high horse?
35 Femininst Jong
37 Picked do
38 Diesel in *Saving Private Ryan*
39 "Telephone Line" rock group
40 Siouan Native American
41 Currier's partner
43 Gave a flush to
45 Performing pairs
46 Hester's was scarlet
48 Wine from noble rot
50 Hillary Clinton's alma mater
51 Former Serbian capital
52 Roland Garros sport
54 Number worn by Johnny Unitas
59 Bone-dry
60 Seine tributary
62 Ingrid's *Casablanca* role
63 Weatherbird
64 Praise lavishly
65 Jay-Z's team
66 Crystal-baller's words
67 Big men on campus
68 "You betcha!"

DOWN

1 Niagara Falls feature
2 Stage actress Menken
3 Santoni in *Dirty Harry*
4 Wanderer
5 Report card notation
6 "Good job!"
7 Worf portrayer Michael
8 Greek letter
9 Anise liqueur
10 Teenage witch Spellman
11 Number worn by Kobe Bryant
12 Place for a ring
13 Composer Speaks
21 Three, in Rome
23 Literary collection
26 Split hairs
27 Martini drop-in
28 Number worn by Wayne Gretzky
29 It has bark but no bite
30 Monk in *The Da Vinci Code*
32 *What the Butler Saw* playwright
33 Symbol of Wild West justice
36 *The Coca-___ Kid* (1985)
42 One of the SRO crowd
43 Decent, so to speak
44 Places for moles
45 It's bound to happen
47 Actor Wallach
49 Railroad beam
52 Kipling's Rikki-tikki-___
53 La Belle Epoch et al.
54 "___ chance!"
55 Not left out of
56 Robert ___ cocktail
57 "Como ___ usted?"
58 "The Ostrich" poet Ogden
61 Give out a pink slip

★ Railways

All the words are hidden vertically, horizontally or diagonally—in both directions. The letters that remain unused form a sentence from left to right.

```
R N U M B E R A I L D W A E Y
N S S M E T S T R I K E W L E
I C E J A T I R E D E V L B E
A L R C U E S C O C O A L A P
R S E O U N T Y K D I N O T Y
T W I N S R C S S E E N C E G
S I L D L S I T S F T A O M N
S T D U E R I T I E F D M I A
E C I C E C E N Y O C A O T T
R H E T P T O G G I N T T H E
P B S O E E N R N T G I I S C
X N E R R I N T R E I N V O O
E G L O L F E A T I S H E E N
N I N P E R C T E E D S N T T
H C U E C K N T U R Y O A A A
S O A I M I N I N G T E R P C
C C T H N I Q C I F F A R T T
U Y E T I C K E T O F F I C E
```

| JUNCTION | LOCOMOTIVE | NUMBER | PASSENGER | SECTION | SECURITY | SIDE-CORRIDOR | SLEEPER | STAFF SYSTEM | STEAM | STRIKE | SWITCH | TICKET | TICKET OFFICE | TIMETABLE | TRACK | TRAFFIC |

COAL	COUPLING	DIESEL
CONDUCTOR	CROSSING	EXPRESS TRAIN
CONTACT	DELAY	INTERCITY

DELETE ONE

Delete one letter from INTRODUCES and get something off.

★★★★ Futoshiki

Fill in the 5 x 5 grid with the numbers from 1 to 5 once per row and column, while following the greater than/lesser than symbols shown. There is only one valid solution that can be reached through logic and clear thinking alone!

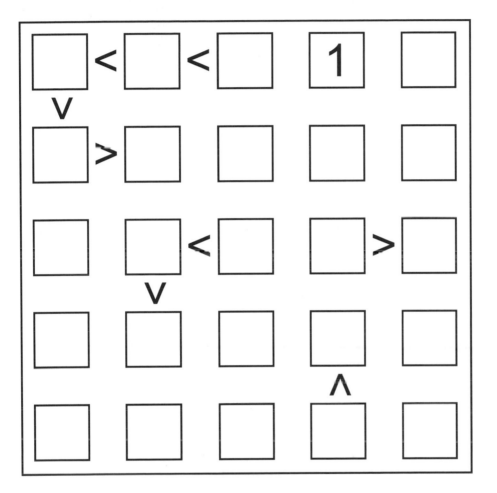

LETTERBLOCKS

Move the letterblocks around so that words are formed on top and below that you can associate with diseases. In one block, the letter from the top row has been switched with the letter from the bottom row.

★★★★★ Castles by Brian O'Shea

ACROSS

1 Juicy pear
5 *Legionnaire* actor Van ___
10 Dark blue
14 *Horton Hears* ___ (2008)
15 Verdi songs
16 Have confidence
17 Blarney Castle locale
19 Either half of Gemini
20 Branagh in *Thor*
21 Countryman
23 "___ y Plata" (Montana motto)
24 It's sprayed in defense
25 Second edition
29 Victor Herbert's *Babes in* ___
32 Burden of proof
33 Bonfire remains
35 *The Time Machine* leisure class
36 Take serious action against
37 Car-towing org.
38 Scottish alder
39 Drops a perfect pass
41 ___ ballerina
43 *As I Lay Dying* father
44 Comes to terms
46 Long and thin
48 City on the Oka River
49 Laptop display
50 Just plain dumb
53 Sundries
57 *CHiPs* star Estrada
58 Hearst Castle locale
60 McCartney's ___ *Cor Meum*
61 Across the keel
62 Dodge model of the 1980s
63 New Mexico ski resort
64 Gallows sight
65 Acute want

DOWN

1 Reverse side
2 "___ is me ...": Ophelia
3 Rebuff
4 McEnroe court rival
5 Florida race place
6 St. Louis landmark
7 "O Sole ___"
8 Painter Chagall
9 Native Alaskans
10 Newspaper submission
11 Larnach Castle locale
12 Netman Nastase
13 Redgrave in *Georgy Girl*
18 Polo in *Little Fockers*
22 River in central Scotland
25 Valentine's Day bunch
26 Harden (to)
27 El Morro Castle locale
28 Winter Palace rulers
29 Sides in a game
30 Swedes' neighbors
31 Place for a short-order cook
34 Japanese affirmative
40 Golfer's count
41 Louisiana's state bird
42 1984 Steve Martin film
43 Firedog
45 Super Bowl IV MVP Dawson
47 Prefix for derm
50 Run into
51 SeaWorld showoff
52 ___ San Lucas (Baja resort)
53 Vardalos and Long
54 "I'm buying!"
55 Number of Beethoven symphonies
56 Stated
59 Neighbor of Virgo

★ Spot the Differences

Find the nine differences in the image on the right.

DOUBLETALK

Homophones are words that share the same pronunciation, no matter how they are spelled. If they are spelled differently then they are called heterographs. Find heterographs meaning:

NOTES PLAYED SIMULTANEOUSLY and ROPE

★★★ BrainSnack®—Chalkface

Which number should replace the question mark?

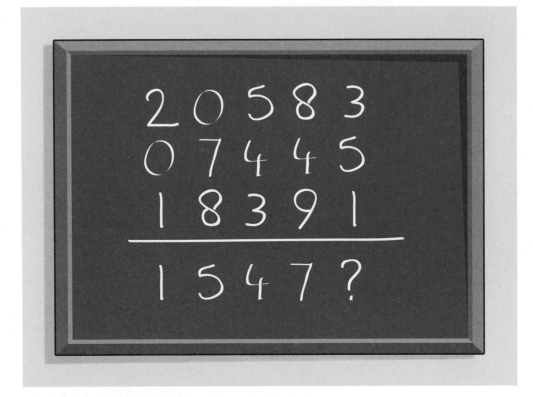

QUICK WORD SEARCH

Find the words associated with gems listed below in the word search grid.

G	O	L	D	S	T	O	N	E	T	I	T	K	E	T
S	P	H	E	N	E	P	H	R	I	T	E	D	A	J
Z	A	A	M	E	T	H	Y	S	T	E	N	R	A	G
I	L	N	A	I	D	I	S	B	O	L	Y	R	E	B
M	O	O	N	S	T	O	N	E	T	I	L	L	E	M

AMETHYST BERYL GARNET GOLDSTONE JADE MELLITE
MOONSTONE NEPHRITE OPAL OBSIDIAN SPHENE TEKTITE

★★★★★ Themeless by John M. Samson

ACROSS

1 Donation
5 Port side
9 Ed in *Too Big to Fail*
14 Niagara Falls sound
15 Scarlett O'Hara's daughter
16 Kind of park
17 *Lost ___ Mancha* (2002)
18 Bondsman's bond
19 Mandel or Long
20 *Long Ago Tomorrow* star
23 La la lead-in
24 "___ the Mood for Love"
25 Leaves in the lurch
29 Got even
32 Love, Spanish-style
33 Chili con ___
35 Epoxy
36 Calendar square
37 DII doubled
38 1975 Frazier opponent
39 Power source
41 Recurrent design
43 Perform without ___
44 Desert delusions
46 Weekend chore, for some
48 Annoying tyke
49 O'Neill sea play
50 Victoria is its capital
58 Plant exudation
59 Home of Hawaii's Pipeline
60 Norse writer Duun
61 Down ___ knee
62 "That makes me mad!"
63 Lost fish of film
64 Minute organism
65 Jane Lynch series
66 McGregor of *The Phantom Menace*

DOWN

1 ___ Reaper
2 Argyll island
3 Halloween season
4 Caterpillar product
5 Matt of *Joey*
6 Jack in *The Rare Breed*
7 *The ___-Flam Man* (1967)
8 Weightlifter's powder
9 Where charity begins
10 Exhibition
11 Pat Patriot is their mascot
12 Biographer Ludwig
13 Line dance
21 Conquistador's quest
22 Jackknife or swan
25 Sir's counterpart
26 Stradivari's mentor
27 "Only the Lonely" singer
28 Birthplace of Pythagoras
29 Smithy's block
30 Noted blind mathematician
31 Vulcan, for one
34 Slower, musically: Abbr.
40 Navratilova of tennis
41 Big Apple team
42 Fiasco
43 Buttercup relative
45 Packed on a few pounds
47 Inuit food cutter
50 Bones of *Sleepy Hollow*
51 Nevada resort
52 Boss on *The Dukes of Hazzard*
53 *Up* protagonist
54 Elbe tributary
55 Gusted
56 "___ Rock": Simon & Garfunkel
57 Bristol river

★★ Sunny Weather

Where will the sun shine? With the knowledge that each arrow points to
a place where a symbol should be, can you locate the sunny spots? The
symbols cannot be next to each other vertically, horizontally or diagonally.
A symbol cannot be placed on top of an arrow. We show one symbol.

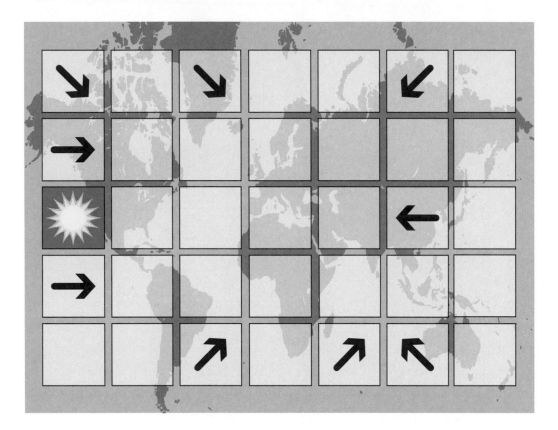

TRIANAGRAM

Three-word groups of anagrams are also called triplets or trianagrams.
Complete the group:

IDEALS   _ _ _ _ _ _   _ _ _ _ _ _

★★★ Binairo

Complete the grid with zeros and ones until there are 5 zeros and 6 ones in every row and every column. No more than two of the same number can be next to or under each other. Rows or columns with exactly the same content are not allowed. There is only one valid solution.

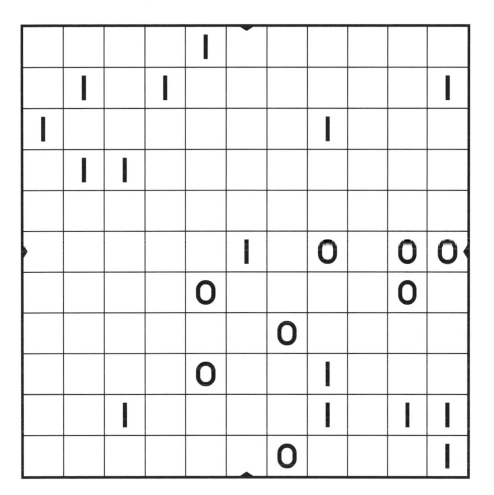

SANDWICH

What four-letter word belongs between the word on the left and the word on the right, so that the first and second word, and the second and third word, each form a common compound word or phrase?

WORK _ _ _ _ KEEPER

★★★ Sudoku

Fill in the grid so that each row, each column and each 3 x 3 frame contains every number from 1 to 9.

		1	4			5		7
	7			2	9	4	6	
6	4	9		5		2		
	6		8			3		
5		4		1				
								9
	8					6		
			3		8			
				6				

SYMBOL SUMS

Can you work out these number sums using three of these four symbols? **+ − ÷ ×**
(No fractions or minus numbers are involved in the sum as you progress from left to right.)

$$19 \,\square\, 3 \,\square\, 2 \,\square\, 3 = 24$$

★★★★★ Themeless by Cindy Wheeler

ACROSS

1 Héctor in *El Cantante*
5 Country 2,880 miles long
10 Spreadsheet filler
14 Fourth person
15 Caches
16 "Oh, golly!"
17 Administration
19 Turkish coin
20 Bring into harmony
21 Outposts
23 *Water for Elephants* novelist Gruen
25 Neur- ending
26 Mighty
30 Signs into law
34 Icelandic letter
35 Caverns of Virginia
37 One who grins and bears it
38 Lays eyes on
40 Tibetan monks
42 Por ___ (therefore)
43 Embers
45 One on a moray foray
47 ___ de mer (seasickness)
48 Undamaged
50 Old Dominion capital
52 Helgenberger in *Erin Brockovich*
54 Small Great Lake
55 Moulin Rouge symbol
59 Necessitate
63 Jacob's hairy brother
64 Where San Juan is
66 Ivy League school
67 Carpenter's tool
68 German-Polish border river
69 Sitar wood
70 Uplift
71 Like the desert of Sinai

DOWN

1 Baby's first word
2 Like ___ out of hell
3 Use U-Haul, e.g.
4 Sentence segment
5 Good-humored
6 That guy
7 "Beware the ___ of March!"
8 At a slow tempo
9 Asheville's Biltmore ___
10 Fragile
11 Exchange fee
12 Cascades lake
13 Some prosecutors, briefly
18 Tree protuberance
22 Cannery row?
24 Halos
26 Joe of *Lethal Weapon 4*
27 "___ a Grecian Urn"
28 Futures commodity
29 Debussy work
31 Kramer of *Seinfeld*
32 Giant moon of Saturn
33 Tongue-lash
36 Bulldog of New Haven
39 Sure thing
41 On the sly
44 Ponzi scheme
46 Ogden Nash's "homely beast"
49 Three-bagger
51 Subways
53 Stuck together, in a way
55 Burst into tears
56 "Of course!"
57 Visitor on *Deep Space Nine*
58 Dolly in *Hello, Dolly!*
60 General's staffer
61 Sweet bakery job?
62 Folk knowledge
65 He may cry foul

★★ Keep Going

Start on a blank square of your choice and connect as many blank squares as possible with one single continuous line. You can only connect squares along vertical and horizontal lines. You must continue the connecting line up until the next obstacle, i.e., the rim of the box, a black square or a square that has already been used. You can change direction at any obstacle you meet. Each square can be used only once. The number of blank squares that will be left unused is marked in the upper square. There is more than one solution. We show only one solution.

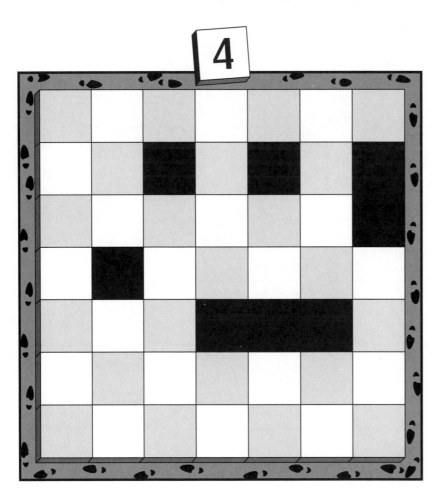

FRIENDS?

What do the following words have in common?

COFFEE CRACK FLESH JACK STOCK FLOWER

★★★ BrainSnack®—Life's a Beach

Which pattern (1–6) should replace the question mark?

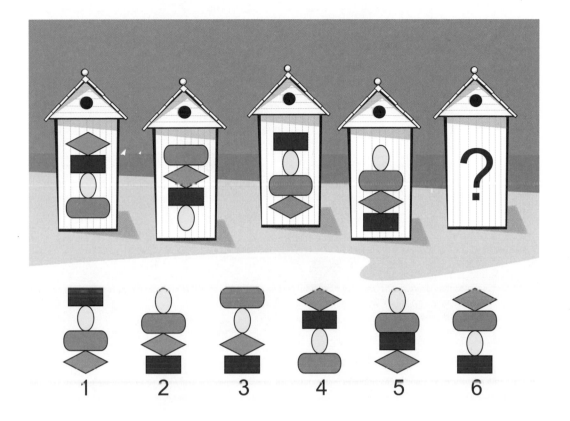

DOODLE PUZZLE

A doodle puzzle is a combination of images, letters and/or numbers that represent a word or a concept. If you cannot solve a doodle puzzle, do not look at the answer right away. Think hard—and outside the box.

★★★★★ Themeless by Linda Lather

ACROSS

1 Zesty flavor
5 Jousting need
10 Prefix for phone
14 Lod Airport carrier
15 Cuzco ancients
16 *Titanic* is one
17 Houston AHL player
18 Collider units
19 Pushed on
20 Fiddler beetle
22 Like some grapes
24 "Got it, daddy-o!"
26 Genetic messenger
27 Leader who fled Tibet in 1959
31 Lake Placid rental
36 Gilbert & Sullivan princess
37 Cleo barged down it
38 Playtime
39 Fisherman's ring wearer
41 Tantalize
43 Debt voucher
44 Prim
46 Golfer Faldo
48 Singer Des'___
49 Busybody
50 Jefferson's veep
52 Musician Severinsen
54 Hook cohort
55 Censure
60 Measly
64 Stuntman Knievel
65 Psychics claim to see them
67 Prefix for tiller
68 "Life for Rent" singer
69 Street urchin
70 Faust sold his
71 Openly concede
72 Serengeti antelope
73 Warhol companion Sedgwick

DOWN

1 English breakfast et al.
2 McCowen in *Gangs of New York*
3 *Cold Case* theme song
4 Attorney Allred
5 No asset
6 Pangolin's morsel
7 E-5 and E-6
8 Pentax product
9 Aalto Theatre city
10 Cry like a baby
11 Fencing sword
12 Cotton machines
13 Bible book
21 Score after deuce
23 Bait fish
25 Howling wind
27 Uncool
28 Be smitten with
29 Rabbit fur
30 "Little Things ___ Lot"
32 Duke's conference
33 India's first prime minister
34 Wicker willow
35 Fragrant compound
38 Endorse
40 "C'___ la vie!"
42 Baronet titles
45 Thompson in *Pollock*
47 Spoon-playing locale
50 Real
51 Amanda of *Married... With Children*
53 Siouan language
55 Mother of Pollux and Helen
56 Tel ___
57 "Love ___": Beatles
58 *Come ___ Your Horn* (1963)
59 Humorist Bombeck
61 *The ___ German* (2006)
62 Fancy sewing case
63 Actor's meat
66 "You Will Be My ___ True Love"

★ Journalism

All the words are hidden vertically, horizontally or diagonally—in both directions. The letters that remain unused form a sentence from left to right.

```
T E L E V I S I O N S A E R J
S P E E D O U R N L A Z T A N
W O B D L I Y C A V I R P D M
E L I S I T O N I R O C M I U
B I L E S T D S P P A G E O L
L T A N O E O R S C O O P S O
O I W H R E E R E R S T H P C
G C P E Q Z Y C S U E M R S T
I S O N T S O A O W W E N H O
R E G I O N T B S E S D E R W
L H L A O S J T I S T I W E D
A U W M E E R V R H F A S U E
P E Y N C A R E S W E N P T S
T R O T I E L E W H E N A E A
O H I N T E R N E T W H P R I
P V I N A N O I T A S N E S B
E N I S N O I S S E F O R P Y
G A E N S C A N D A L D H O W
```

POLITICS
PRESS RELEASE
PRIVACY
PROFESSION
PULITZER PRIZE
RADIO
REGION
REUTERS
SCANDAL
SCOOP
SENSATION
SLANDER
SPEED
SPORT
TELEVISION
TRAINING
WEBLOG

BIASED
COLUMN
ECONOMY
EDITORS
ESSAY

HONEST
INTERNET
INTERVIEW
LAPTOP
LIBEL

MEDIA
NEWS
NEWSPAPER
OBJECTIVE
PHOTO

DELETE ONE

Delete one letter from LATITUDES and go higher.

★★★ Sport Maze

Draw the shortest way from the ball to the goal. You can only move along vertical and horizontal lines, not along diagonal lines. The figure on each square indicates the number of squares the ball must be moved in the same direction. You can change direction at each stop.

5	3	4	5	2	1
4	3	1	1	4	3
⚪2	3	0	0	1	4
4	3	3	1	4	5
1	3	2	2	3	2
4	5	⚪	1	4	1

ONE LETTER LESS OR MORE

The word on the right side contains the letters of the word on the left side plus or minus the letter in the middle. One letter is already in the right place.

O P E R A T O R +C ☐ ☐ R ☐ ☐ ☐ ☐ ☐ ☐

★★★★★ Themeless by Karen Peterson

ACROSS

1 Tyrrhenian Sea isle
5 Black-and-white duck
9 Turned off the sound
14 Obstreperous
15 Top of the heap
16 Asinine
17 Like pay-TV signals
19 Sorta
20 Field of touchdowns?
21 Goof-off
23 Cher's *Clueless* friend
24 *Deep Space Nine* changeling
25 Rabbit ears
29 Entrance-level position?
33 Uncool one
34 Confederate of Aramis
36 Part of n.b.
37 ___ Lanka
38 MapQuest's owner
39 Carried out
40 Smooth
42 Flower
44 Game before a final
45 Rhapsodic
47 Sidewinder
49 "___ we meet again"
50 1958 Mideast alliance
51 Took in
55 Fan club member
59 Diameter halves
60 It's often deleted
62 *The Honeymooners* role
63 Virna in *Arabella*
64 Lawrence Durrell novel
65 Coastal golf course
66 Property claim
67 Caribou group

DOWN

1 Lioness in *Born Free*
2 Central sites
3 Raymond in *Rear Window*
4 Like some screenplays
5 Kate's *Charlie's Angels* role
6 Shed
7 67.5° on the compass
8 Ties the knot
9 Yum-Yum's sovereign
10 Ark misser of song
11 Combat vehicle
12 *The Neverending Story* author
13 Letter opener
18 Ghostly sound
22 *Gigi* playwright
25 Photographer Adams
26 Brazen
27 Sampler
28 "Any Time ___": Beatles
29 Sorrow
30 Heidi Klum, for one
31 "And ___ to every purpose ...": Eccl. 3:1
32 Rock bottom
35 "Yoo-___!"
41 Quibble
42 Cotton bundle
43 Schmaltzy
44 Elaine in *Small Time Crooks*
46 Norman and Eugene, e.g.
48 Hardly feisty
51 Shrinking Asian sea
52 "The Persistence of Memory" painter
53 Thor's father
54 Inspiron computer
55 Basilica feature
56 Make hopping mad
57 "Be it ___ so humble ..."
58 Check for typos
61 Highest clock number

★ Word Sudoku

Complete the grid so that each row, each column and each 3 x 3 frame contains the nine letters from the black box below. The hidden nine-letter word is in the diagonal from top left to bottom right.

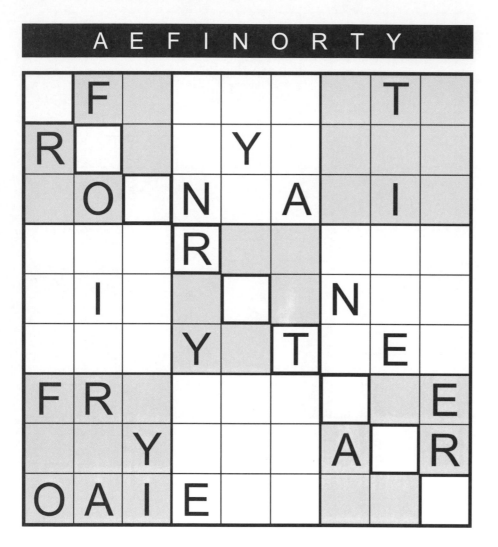

| A | E | F | I | N | O | R | T | Y |

UNCANNY TURN

Rearrange the letters of the phrase below to form a cognate anagram, one which is related or connected in meaning to the original phrase. The answer can be one or more words.

DEVOUR HORSES

★ Cage the Animals

Draw lines to completely divide up the grid into small squares with exactly one animal per square. The squares should not overlap.

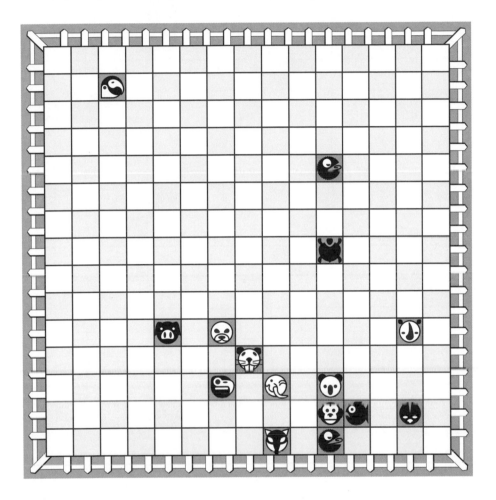

WORD WALL

Beginning at the left side of the wall, make a word by adding one group of letters from each column as you move left to right. When you have found the first word, go back to the second column and start the next word, gathering one group of letters from each column, and so on until all the letters are used to make six words.

★★★★★ Themeless by Maggie Ellis

ACROSS

1 Italia capital
5 Clubs for Rory McIlroy
10 Not us
14 Asia's Trans-___ mountain range
15 Summer camp craft
16 Cut some slack
17 *Glengarry Glen Ross* star
19 "That's too bad!"
20 Lacking strength
21 Word for an ultrasaurus
23 Prefix for highest
25 Greek Amor
26 Comical to the max
30 Junk rooms
34 Plaza de toros cry
35 Wordless
37 Eagle nest
38 Designer de la Fressange
40 "___, I'm Adam"
42 Four-star review
43 Big dipper
45 Make good on a debt
47 *The Glass Key* hero Beaumont
48 Cookie Monster's street
50 Peace of mind
52 They close at night
54 Coating of ice
55 Madrid miss
59 Little sample
63 Jack Horner's find
64 "One Boy, One Girl" singer
66 Errand runner
67 Tribal symbol on a pole
68 Raison d'___
69 Nettled (with "off")
70 English china
71 Title page?

DOWN

1 Indian royal
2 Jones in *American Virgin*
3 Nutmeg spice
4 MVP of Super Bowl XXVII
5 Baked Alaska ingredient
6 Aries is one
7 A-ha's "Take ___"
8 Nary a soul
9 Madrid missus
10 Trucker
11 Saintly symbol
12 Jacob's Biblical twin
13 Jumble
18 Okay legally
22 Catholic tribunal
24 Muppet in a trash can
26 Olympic weapons
27 Forearm bones
28 Musts
29 Moon-related phenomena
31 Ayatollah follower
32 Source of musk
33 Shabby and untidy
36 Slender candle
39 Zigzagged downhill
41 Seafaring
44 Royal Arabian
46 Neighbor of Oman
49 Royal decrees
51 Got close
53 Brownstone porch
55 Soon-forgotten quarrel
56 Art historian Faure
57 Without a stitch
58 k.d. lang's voice
60 Malaysian skewered dish
61 Australia's largest lake
62 Wetlands plant
65 TV type

★★★ BrainSnack®—Shapes

Which stack (A or B) should be added and in which position (1–3)? Answer like this: 1B.

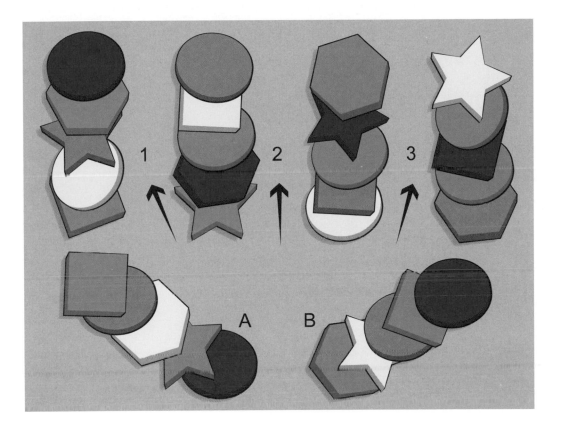

BLOCK ANAGRAM

Form the word that is described in the brackets with the letters above the grid. An extra letter is already in the right place.

POLISH HERO (investigator of questions about existence)

P										

★ Safe Code

To open the safe you have to replace the question mark with the correct figure. You can find this figure by determining the logical method behind the numbers shown. These methods can include calculation, inversion, repetition, chronological succession, or forming ascending and descending series.

SAFE A08

DOODLE PUZZLE

A doodle puzzle is a combination of images, letters and/or numbers that represent a word or a concept. If you cannot solve a doodle puzzle, do not look at the answer right away. Think hard—and outside the box.

★★★★★ Themeless by John M. Samson

ACROSS
1 Grapefruit portion
5 *The Pilot's Wife* author Shreve
10 Bring up
14 Olive genus
15 The Jetsons' maid
16 Rochester's love
17 Creeping flesh
19 Act the pawnbroker
20 Bear up under
21 Gave strength to
23 Suffix meaning "to the max"
24 Dominant (male)
25 Lying face down
29 State that borders Nepal
33 Go ballistic
34 Technique
35 Not volatile
36 "___ Now or Never": Presley
37 Places for pinballers
39 Answer to the Sphinx riddle
40 Amontillado, for one
42 One with a record
43 AT&T Park locale
44 Allots
45 Gloss over
47 Hunting knife
49 Hot time for Nancy
50 Nine-day prayers
53 Ham's need
57 With, en français
58 Teaching asset
60 "Othello" piece
61 Fail to say clearly
62 Book of the Book of Mormon
63 Nick and Nora's pet
64 Metric force units
65 Hard to come by

DOWN
1 Sty animals
2 1966 N.L. batting champ
3 Early August babies
4 Tops in celerity
5 Selected at random
6 Proper name
7 Suffix with hero
8 Frequent the pubs
9 "The Lion and the Mouse" fabulist
10 Discharge
11 Looker
12 *Artaxerxes* composer
13 *Sanford and Son* star Foxx
18 Sunrise direction
22 "___ the occasion?"
24 Case handled by a lawyer?
25 Parallelepiped
26 Early-blooming
27 First sign
28 Compass doodle
30 Island studied by Margaret Mead
31 "Lonely Nights" singer Bryan
32 Talking bird
35 Life and death, for two
37 Flaming felony
38 "Where ___ sign?"
41 Miss Randall of Sunnybrook Farm
43 "Kisses ___ Than Wine"
45 How King Solomon ruled
46 Sundance's woman
48 Got one's ankles wet
50 Zilch
51 Sheep genus
52 Waistcoat
53 Campaign worker
54 ABBA's ballerina
55 Wife of Hussein I
56 *As I Lay Dying* father
59 Background noise

★ Word Pyramid

Each word in the pyramid has the letters of the word above it, plus a new letter.

T
(1) in the direction of
(2) large amount
(3) unable to be found
(4) took secretly
(5) inexpensive lodging place for travelers
(6) leather case for a pistol
(7) tunnels made by vermin

DOUBLETALK

Homophones are words that share the same pronunciation, no matter how they are spelled. If they are spelled differently then they are called heterographs. Find heterographs meaning:

CIRCUITS and EXPIRE

★ Hourglass

Starting in the middle, each word in the top half has the letters of the word below it, plus a new letter, and each word in the bottom half has the letters of the word above it, plus a new letter.

(1) less visible
(2) origin
(3) invoke evil upon
(4) consumer

(5) certain
(6) caretaker
(7) protect against risk
(8) dawn

UNCANNY TURN

Rearrange the letters of the phrase below to form a cognate anagram, one which is related or connected in meaning to the original phrase. The answer can be one or more words.

TUMBLES

★ Monkey Business

Some of the older students have been monkeying about with the BEST KIDS BOOKS titles list in the library. Can you fix it?

1 NIGHTS WEAK WORTHY
    by David Macaulay
2 STOIC WINNIE-THE-POOH DOODLES
    by Laurie Keller
3 HOLLOW MUSICIAN HIM
    by David M. Schwartz
4 HOSANNA NOW TUBBY AGITATOR
    by Kathy Darling
5 SUAVENESS CROONING FAT UNTRUE HERO
    by Annie Jones

TRIANAGRAM

Three-word groups of anagrams are also called triplets or trianagrams.
Complete the group:

LEMONS   _ _ _ _ _ _   _ _ _ _ _ _

PAGE 15
By Jiminy!

F	O	A	L		U	L	N	A		H	I	J	A	B
I	D	L	E		N	E	O	N		U	S	A	G	E
J	I	M	B	O	K	E	R	N		D	O	M	E	S
I	N	S	A	N	E	R		E	N	D	L	E	S	S
			N	I	P			O	L	D	S			
R	E	J	E	C	T	S		S	W	E	E	T	E	R
A	N	I	S	E		K	N	E	A	D		K	E	Y
D	A	M	E		D	A	N	N	Y		B	I	R	D
A	T	M		P	A	L	E	D		M	A	R	I	E
R	E	Y	N	A	R	D		S	P	A	N	K	E	R
			W	O	R	E			A	N	D			
A	L	A	M	E	D	A		A	S	S	A	I	L	S
F	E	L	O	N		J	I	M	H	E	N	S	O	N
A	V	E	R	T		A	R	I	A		A	L	V	A
R	I	S	E	S		R	E	D	S		S	E	E	P

PAGE 16
BrainSnack®—Family Ties

Butterfly C. Red, green and blue are the other three family colors.

CHANGELINGS

P R O D U C T I V E
E X C E L L E N C E
S U C C E S S F U L

PAGE 17
Belgian Beers

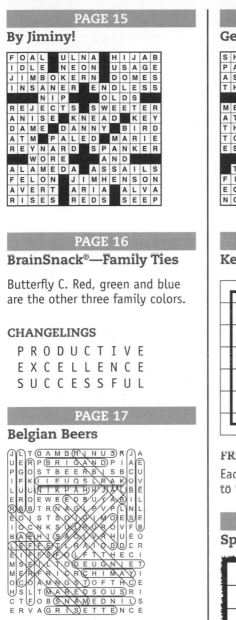

Trappist beer is brewed by Trappists, monks of the Order of the Cistercians of the Strict Observance.

DELETE ONE
Delete A and find MENTION

PAGE 18
George Clooney

S	H	A	H		C	R	E	E	D		W	R	I	T
P	A	N	E		H	O	R	D	E		H	A	R	E
A	S	T	A		A	T	S	E	A		E	P	I	C
T	H	E	D	E	S	C	E	N	D	A	N	T	S	
			L	E	T			B	R	C				
M	E	D	A	L	E	D		R	O	B	E	R	T	S
A	T	O	M		E	M	I	L	Y		O	H	A	
T	H	E	P	E	R	F	E	C	T	S	T	O	R	M
T	O	R		N	O	O	N	E		S	T	E	M	
E	S	S	E	N	C	E		R	E	B	U	S	E	S
			Y	U	K			F	U	N				
	T	H	E	I	D	E	S	O	F	M	A	R	C	H
F	I	E	F		O	V	A	T	E		M	A	R	E
E	C	R	U		V	I	N	I	C		I	R	O	N
N	O	E	L		E	L	E	C	T		S	E	W	S

PAGE 19
Keep Going

FRIENDS?
Each can have the prefix CONTRA- to form a new word.

PAGE 20
Sport Maze

ONE LETTER LESS OR MORE
TRANSPIRE

PAGE 21
Dynamic Duos

L	O	A	M		R	U	R	A	L		S	C	A	D
B	R	I	E		E	N	O	L	A		A	H	O	Y
J	A	N	A	N	D	D	E	A	N		L	I	N	E
			S	O	H	O		S	T	O	O	P	E	D
A	S	T	U	T	E			E	N	N	A			
T	H	O	R	E	A	U		D	R	A	G	N	E	T
T	A	M	E		T	R	A	I	N		A	D	D	S
U	M	A			G	I	N			D	I	E		
N	A	N	S		F	E	T	E	D		T	A	C	T
E	N	D	E	A	R	S		R	E	S	U	L	T	S
			J	A	D	E		C	H	E	E	S	E	
B	L	E	S	S	E	D		P	L	U	S			
A	E	R	I		M	I	K	E	A	N	D	I	K	E
B	A	R	D		A	N	E	A	R		A	R	I	L
A	R	Y	E		N	O	L	T	E		Y	A	N	K

PAGE 22
BrainSnack®—Skewered

Kebab 5. All the other kebabs have a sausage at both ends.

LETTER LINE
CHANGEOVER; GOVERN, HAVOC, CHEVRON, CHARGE, HANGER

PAGE 23
Word Sudoku

A	Y	R	S	T	O	J	L	G
L	S	G	Y	R	J	T	O	A
O	J	T	G	L	A	R	Y	S
G	L	Y	R	S	T	A	J	O
T	R	J	A	O	Y	G	S	L
S	A	O	J	G	L	Y	R	T
J	G	A	L	Y	S	O	T	R
Y	O	L	T	A	R	S	G	J
R	T	S	O	J	G	L	A	Y

UNCANNY TURN
NORWEGIANS

PAGE 24
Loves

PAGE 25
Sudoku

9	7	5	6	4	2	1	3	8
2	3	1	9	7	8	4	5	6
4	6	8	1	5	3	9	7	2
5	1	3	2	9	7	6	8	4
8	9	6	5	1	4	3	2	7
7	2	4	3	8	6	5	9	1
6	4	2	8	3	5	7	1	9
1	5	7	4	2	9	8	6	3
3	8	9	7	6	1	2	4	5

SYMBOL SUMS
4 x 3 - 3 ÷ 3 = 3

PAGE 26
Sunny Weather

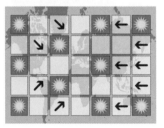

TRIANAGRAM
SILVER, SLIVER

PAGE 27
Flower Girls

L	E	T	A		O	R	A	L	E		I	T	I	S
A	M	A	D		H	Y	S	O	N		M	I	S	S
P	E	T	U	N	I	A		P	I	G		I	G	E	T
S	E	A	L	I	O	N		S	I	S	T	E	R	S
E	R	R	A	T	A			N	E	A	R			
		T	A	N	G		S	E	T	T	L	E	R	
B	E	D	E		S	I	F	T	S		E	I	N	E
A	D	A			G	I	A			L	T	S		
L	E	I	S		A	O	R	T	A		N	Y	E	T
I	N	S	T	A	N	T		E	S	M	E			
	Y	A	R	D			C	A	S	T	L	E	
A	N	D	R	O	I	D		P	E	R	T	A	I	N
T	O	U	T		R	O	S	E	N	Y	L	U	N	D
L	I	K	E		O	G	L	E	D		E	P	E	E
I	R	E	D		N	E	O	N	S		S	E	N	D

PAGE 28
Futoshiki

4	3	5	2	1
3	5	1	4	2
1	4	2	3	5
2	1	4 < 5	3
5	2 < 3	1	4

LETTERBLOCKS
MINOLTA
OLYMPUS

PAGE 29
BrainSnack®—Just Desserts

Container 3. The color of vowels and consonants differs in all the other containers.

QUICK CROSSWORD

A	U	S	T	R	I	A				S		Q
	Y			P		L		C	A	N	A	D	A
	R	U	S	S	I	A		H		M		T
	I						O	M	A	N		O		A
G	A	B	O	N		S		D		A		R

PAGE 30
Hobbies

Hobbies are pursued out of interest, not as paid work; they are done for pleasure.

DELETE ONE
Delete I and find OPENER

PAGE 31
2012 Winners

T	A	O	S		E	D	N	A		S	L	A	T	E
A	C	M	E		N	A	I	L		P	I	N	O	N
T	H	E	A	R	T	I	S	T		I	N	D	R	I
S	E	N	S	O	R	S		O	N	E	E	Y	E	D
			H	O	E			A	L	U	M			
I	N	J	O	K	E	S		S	T	E	P	U	P	S
S	O	U	R	S		N	O	M	A	D		R	O	C
N	O	S	E		L	A	P	E	L		O	R	S	O
E	S	T		A	O	R	T	A		A	V	A	S	T
R	E	I	S	S	U	E		R	E	D	E	Y	E	S
			N	E	S	S			N	O	R			
P	A	R	T	I	E	S		S	C	R	A	P	E	S
H	O	O	T	S		K	A	N	Y	E	W	E	S	T
I	N	S	E	T		E	G	I	S		E	A	S	E
L	E	E	R	S		W	E	P	T		D	R	E	W

PAGE 32
Spot the Differences

DOUBLETALK
PRAISE/PRAYS

PAGE 33
Sudoku X

8	3	2	6	5	1	4	9	7
4	7	6	9	3	8	5	1	2
5	9	1	4	2	7	8	3	6
6	8	3	2	1	9	7	4	5
1	2	4	7	6	5	9	8	3
9	5	7	3	8	4	2	6	1
7	1	5	8	9	6	3	2	4
3	4	9	1	7	2	6	5	8
2	6	8	5	4	3	1	7	9

BLOCK ANAGRAM
ASTRONOMER

PAGE 34
Alphabet Trios

A	L	L	A		C	O	A	T		M	O	D	E	M
L	A	O	S		O	R	L	E		A	R	E	N	A
E	D	D	S		N	C	A	A		R	A	F	T	S
X	Y	Z	A	F	F	A	I	R		I	N	L	E	T
		U	R	I			I	N	G	E				
A	B	A	L	O	N	E		S	T	E	E	P	L	E
D	E	B	T		E	R	G	O	T		S	P	A	S
A	R	C		W	I	L			A	C	T			
M	E	N	S		L	I	L	A	C		C	R	E	E
S	T	E	T	S	O	N		N	O	B	O	D	Y	S
	T	R	I	P			M	O	M					
R	O	W	A	N		K	L	M	F	L	I	G	H	T
A	L	O	N	G		N	O	L	O		C	R	E	W
M	E	R	G	E		E	M	I	R		A	E	R	I
S	A	K	E	S		W	A	I	T		L	Y	O	N

PAGE 35
BrainSnack®—Numbers Game

4 appears six times.

QUICK WORD SEARCH

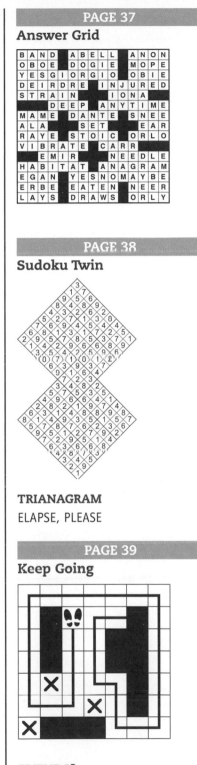

PAGE 36
Kakuro

4	5	7			7	3	2
8	6	9			8	5	6
3		1	5	6	2	3	
		7	6	9		1	
9	5			3	2		
6	1		7	1	2	4	
7	9	6			5	8	9

DOUBLETALK
STAKE/STEAK

PAGE 37
Answer Grid

B	A	N	D		A	B	E	L	L		A	N	O	N
O	B	O	E		D	O	G	I	E		M	O	P	E
Y	E	S	G	I	O	R	G	I	O		O	B	I	E
D	E	I	R	D	R	E		I	N	J	U	R	E	D
S	T	R	A	I	N			I	O	N	A			
			D	E	E	P		A	N	Y	T	I	M	E
M	A	M	E		D	A	N	T	E		S	N	E	E
A	L	A		S	E	T			E	A	R			
R	A	Y	E		S	T	O	I	C		O	R	L	O
V	I	B	R	A	T	E		C	A	R	R			
	E	M	I	R			N	E	E	D	L	E		
H	A	B	I	T	A	T		A	N	A	G	R	A	M
E	G	A	N		Y	E	S	N	O	M	A	Y	B	E
E	R	B	E		E	A	T	E	N		N	E	E	R
L	A	Y	S		D	R	A	W	S		O	R	L	Y

PAGE 38
Sudoku Twin

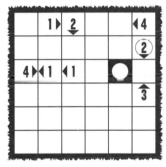

TRIANAGRAM
ELAPSE, PLEASE

PAGE 39
Keep Going

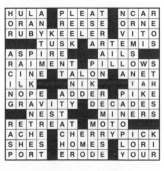

FRIENDS?
Each can have the prefix UNDER-
to form a new word.

PAGE 40
Black and White

W	A	L	L		S	P	A	S	M		A	D	A	M
A	L	E	E		H	E	L	L	O		L	E	N	A
L	I	M	A		A	S	P	E	R		O	M	A	R
S	K	U	N	K		T	H	E	A	R	T	I	S	T
H	E	R	O	E	S		P	S	I					
			N	A	T	A	L		S	C	A	L	E	S
S	O	L		E	L	O	I			E	D	I	L	E
C	R	O	S	S	W	O	R	D	P	U	Z	Z	L	E
A	C	O	R	N		E	N	O	L		A	S	K	
D	A	M	S	E	L		A	L	O	F	T			
			V	I	P		D	E	S	I	G	N		
D	A	L	M	A	T	I	A	N		Z	E	B	R	A
I	G	O	R		E	P	S	O	M		T	S	A	R
S	U	R	E		R	E	T	R	O		S	E	N	D
H	E	E	D		S	T	A	M	P		E	N	D	O

PAGE 41
Sport Maze

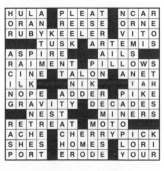

ONE LETTER LESS OR MORE
INTENSE

PAGE 42
BrainSnack®—True Romance

Mary. The two names of each couple contain the same vowels.

DOODLE PUZZLE
MAsks

PAGE 43
Reds

H	U	L	A		P	L	E	A	T		N	C	A	R
O	R	A	N		R	E	E	S	E		O	R	N	E
R	U	B	Y	K	E	E	L	E	R		V	I	T	O
			T	U	S	K		A	R	T	E	M	I	S
A	S	P	I	R	E			A	I	L	S			
R	A	I	M	E	N	T		P	I	L	L	O	W	S
C	I	N	E		T	A	L	O	N		A	N	E	T
I	L	K			N	I	K			T	A	R		
N	O	P	E		A	D	D	E	R		P	I	K	E
G	R	A	V	I	T	Y		D	E	C	A	D	E	S
			N	E	S	T		M	I	N	E	R	S	
R	E	T	R	E	A	T		M	O	T	O			
A	C	H	E		C	H	E	R	R	Y	P	I	C	K
S	H	E	S		H	O	M	E	S		L	O	R	I
P	O	R	T		E	R	O	D	E		Y	O	U	R

PAGE 44

Tea

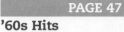

When the English have afternoon tea, they drink very strong tea with lots of milk and sugar.

DELETE ONE

Delete S and find INVESTIGATOR

PAGE 45

Word Sudoku

C	A	E	I	M	D	O	T	X
D	O	I	X	T	A	E	M	C
T	X	M	E	C	O	D	I	A
I	D	O	M	A	E	C	X	T
E	T	X	O	I	C	A	D	M
A	M	C	D	X	T	I	O	E
X	I	D	A	E	M	T	C	O
O	C	A	T	D	X	M	E	I
M	E	T	C	O	I	X	A	D

UNCANNY TURN

PITTANCE

PAGE 46

Binairo

0	I	I	0	I	I	0	0	I	I	0	0
I	0	I	0	I	0	I	0	I	I	0	0
0	I	0	I	0	0	I	I	0	0	I	I
I	0	0	I	0	I	0	I	0	I	0	I
0	I	I	0	I	I	0	0	I	0	I	0
0	0	I	0	I	0	I	I	0	I	I	0
I	I	0	I	0	I	0	0	I	0	0	I
I	0	0	I	I	0	I	0	0	I	0	I
0	I	I	0	0	I	I	0	0	I	0	I
I	0	0	I	I	0	0	I	I	0	0	I
I	I	0	I	0	0	I	0	0	I	I	0
0	0	I	0	0	I	0	I	I	0	I	I

SYMBOL SUMS

$9 ÷ 3 + 5 \times 6 = 48$

PAGE 47

'60s Hits

PAGE 48

Horoscope

WORD WALL

AUTOBIOGRAPHICALLY, DISHEARTENINGLY, ANTAGONISTIC CALCULATE, DEMONS, ART

PAGE 49

BrainSnack®—Shaping

Shape 3. All the other shapes are divided in equal parts white and black.

TRIANAGRAM

BREAK, BRAKE

PAGE 50

'70s Hits

PAGE 51

Sudoku

4	1	5	6	8	3	9	2	7
9	8	2	5	4	7	3	6	1
6	3	7	9	1	2	8	4	5
8	7	4	1	6	9	5	3	2
2	6	3	7	5	4	1	8	9
5	9	1	3	2	8	6	7	4
1	4	6	2	3	5	7	9	8
7	5	8	4	9	6	2	1	3
3	2	9	8	7	1	4	5	6

SYMBOL SUMS

$8 \times 3 + 9 ÷ 3 = 11$

PAGE 52

Number Cluster

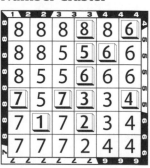

SANDWICH

CHAIR

PAGE 53
'80s Hits

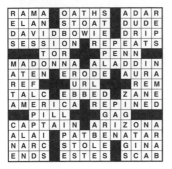

PAGE 54
Concentration—Place 100

Letter D

LETTER LINE

DECORATORS; ROOSTER, COASTER, REACTORS, CREATOR, CEDAR

PAGE 55
BrainSnack®—Runaway Train

Shadow 3. On 1 the wheels are too far apart. 2 has less smoke. On 4 the chimney has been moved and on 5 the window is not in the right place.

CHANGELINGS

C L E V E R N E S S
D E D I C A T I O N
C O N F I D E N C E

PAGE 56
'90s Hits

PAGE 57
Fast Food

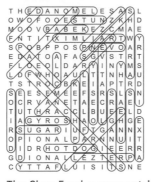

The Slow Food movement is opposed to fast food and wants to preserve traditional and regional cuisine.

DELETE ONE

Delete S and find THE GAME OF BILLIARDS

PAGE 58
Sunny Weather

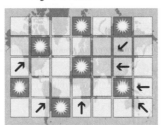

TRIANAGRAM

RUDEST, RUSTED

PAGE 59
'00s Hits

PAGE 60
Keep Going

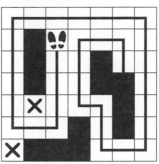

FRIENDS?

Each can have the prefix BLUE to form a new word.

PAGE 61
Sports Maze

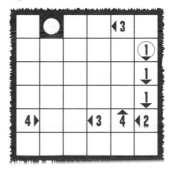

ONE LETTER LESS OR MORE

WELFARE

PAGE 62
Sticks and Stones

PAGE 63
BrainSnack®—Axe Man

6. All other guitars have one fret more on the neck.

DOUBLETALK
STATIONERY/STATIONARY

PAGE 64
Word Sudoku

W	D	U	E	L	I	O	R	G
L	O	I	D	G	R	E	W	U
G	E	R	U	W	O	L	I	D
I	W	D	L	O	G	U	E	R
E	R	O	I	D	U	W	G	L
U	L	G	R	E	W	D	O	I
O	U	E	G	R	D	I	L	W
R	I	L	W	U	E	G	D	O
D	G	W	O	I	L	R	U	E

UNCANNY TURN
POINT

PAGE 65
Binairo

O	I	O	O	I	I	I	O	I	O	I	I
I	I	O	I	O	I	I	I	O	I	O	O
I	O	I	I	O	O	I	I	I	O	I	O
O	I	I	O	I	I	O	I	O	I	O	O
I	I	O	I	I	O	I	O	I	O	I	O
I	O	I	I	O	I	O	I	O	O	I	I
O	O	I	O	I	O	I	I	O	I	O	I
O	I	O	I	O	I	O	I	I	O	I	I
I	I	O	O	I	O	I	O	I	O	I	O
I	O	I	I	O	O	I	O	O	I	I	I
O	O	I	O	I	I	I	O	I	I	O	I

SANDWICH
CART

PAGE 66
Stormy Weather

PAGE 67
Cage the Animals

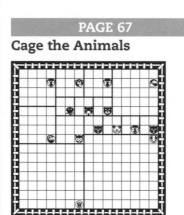

WORD WALL
DISPROPORTIONALITY, AUTHENTICATIONS, ACCELERATION, CHAMPAGNE, DRIVER, IVY

PAGE 68
BrainSnack®—Spokes

Rider 8. The riders finish one team at a time with the lowest number in the team first and the others in ascending order.

QUICK WORD SEARCH

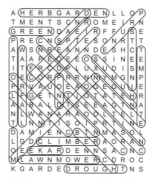

PAGE 69
Hoofers

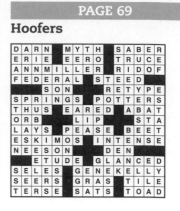

PAGE 70
Garden

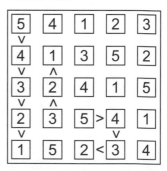

Allotments come in different sorts and shapes, including vegetable gardens, ornamental gardens and rock gardens.

DELETE ONE
Delete E and find GRAND FINAL

PAGE 71
Futoshiki

5	4	1	2	3
4	1	3	5	2
3	2	4	1	5
2	3	5	4	1
1	5	2	3	4

LETTERBLOCKS
CONQUER
CAPTURE

PAGE 72
Hard Stuff

R	O	T	C		S	I	G	M	A		A	P	O	D
B	R	I	O		C	R	A	I	G		L	U	R	E
I	R	O	N	M	A	I	D	E	N		G	M	A	N
		F	A	T	S		N	O	R	E	P	L	Y	
I	N	S	U	L	T			M	A	R	I			
R	A	T	T	L	E	R		R	E	M	I	N	D	S
O	G	E	E		R	A	M	O	N		A	G	E	E
N	A	E			C	O	B				I	V	E	
I	N	L	A		D	E	P	O	T		B	R	I	M
C	O	W	B	O	Y	S		T	H	E	R	O	S	E
	H	A	W	N			R	A	I	N	E	D		
S	T	E	L	L	A	R		M	I	T	T			
A	R	E	O		M	A	N	O	F	S	T	E	E	L
K	I	L	N		I	N	E	R	T		L	E	V	Y
I	P	S	E		C	A	T	T	Y		E	L	A	N

PAGE 73
Spot the Differences

DOODLE PUZZLE
Female (F-email)

PAGE 74
BrainSnack®—Big Game

563412. All the other ticker numbers are combinations of the numbers 12, 34 and 56 and 563412 is the last possible combination of these numbers.

LETTER LINE
NOTICEABLY; BOTANIC, BALCONY, NOTABLE, NOBLE, BOAT

PAGE 75
High Spirits

A	H	A	B		C	R	O	A	K		S	T	O	P
N	A	V	I		A	I	S	L	E		A	H	S	O
T	H	E	G	I	N	G	A	M	E		R	E	E	L
		S	C	A	G		A	P	P	A	R	E	L	
H	A	S	H	E	S			S	U	L	U			
E	S	C	O	R	T	S		D	I	L	E	M	M	A
A	L	O	T		A	C	T	O	N		E	D	A	S
R	E	T			R	I	D				I	N	S	
S	E	C	T		F	U	N	G	I		R	A	N	I
E	P	H	R	A	I	M		E	N	C	O	R	E	S
	B	A	R	R			L	A	D	Y	D	I		
D	E	R	I	D	E	S		D	A	M	E			
U	P	O	N		B	O	U	R	B	O	N	R	E	D
M	I	T	E		U	R	A	N	O		T	A	X	I
A	C	H	E		G	A	B	O	R		S	T	E	M

PAGE 76
Safe Code

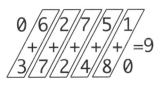

$$\frac{0}{3} + \frac{6}{7} + \frac{2}{2} + \frac{7}{4} + \frac{5}{8} + \frac{1}{0} = 9$$

SANDWICH
BRUSH

PAGE 77
Word Pyramid

(1) SE, (2) set, (3) nest, (4) stern, (5) insert, (6) stinger, (7) integers

DOUBLETALK
WADE/WEIGHED

PAGE 78
Sudoku

6	1	4	7	5	8	9	2	3
5	8	9	1	3	2	4	7	6
7	3	2	9	6	4	8	5	1
2	4	6	5	8	7	1	3	9
3	9	7	2	1	6	5	4	8
1	5	8	4	9	3	2	6	7
4	2	1	3	7	9	6	8	5
8	7	5	6	2	1	3	9	4
9	6	3	8	4	5	7	1	2

SYMBOL SUMS
19 - 3 ÷ 2 x 3 = 24

PAGE 79
Rita and Company

A	N	G	S	T		D	A	B	O		M	I	C	A
D	E	L	T	A		A	G	A	L		A	S	O	N
A	V	E	R	T		C	A	R	Y	G	R	A	N	T
M	A	N	A	T	E	E		I	M	I	T	A	T	E
		N	Y	E	T			P	R	I	C	E	S	
I	N	F	E	R	N	O		K	I	L	N			
R	O	O	D		A	G	O	R	A		A	J	A	R
M	E	R			D	O	O				O	R	O	
A	L	D	O		L	E	O	N	A		P	H	I	L
		P	L	A	N		A	R	S	E	N	A	L	
P	E	P	P	E	R			T	H	A	W			
A	V	E	R	A	G	E		S	E	E	S	A	W	S
G	E	N	E	K	E	L	L	Y		L	O	Y	A	L
E	R	N	S		S	K	I	N		L	U	N	G	E
D	Y	E	S		T	E	T	E		S	P	E	E	D

PAGE 80
Keep Going

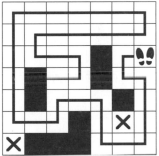

FRIENDS?
Each can have the prefix BUSH- to form a new word.

PAGE 81
BrainSnack®—At the Movies

22. The number between the letters equals the sum of the place of these numbers in the alphabet. 17 (Q) + 5 (E) = 22.

WORD WALL
GASTROENTEROLOGIST, PROFESSIONALISM, PEACEFULNESS CONFIDENT, BREEZE, FAN

PAGE 82
Scrap Heap

PAGE 83
Cooking Techniques

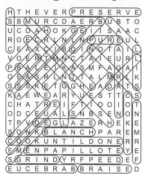

The verb "to cook" is a collective term for all the ways that food can be prepared.

DELETE ONE
Delete A and find THE DENTIST

PAGE 84
Sport Maze

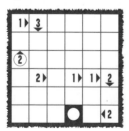

ONE LETTER LESS OR MORE
LANDING

PAGE 85
The Odd Trio

PAGE 86
Word Sudoku

E	A	B	D	S	P	N	Q	L
D	S	N	Q	B	L	E	A	P
Q	L	P	E	N	A	D	S	B
P	Q	E	L	D	S	B	N	A
N	B	S	P	A	E	Q	L	D
A	D	L	B	Q	N	P	E	S
B	E	D	S	L	Q	A	P	N
S	P	A	N	E	B	L	D	Q
L	N	Q	A	P	D	S	B	E

UNCANNY TURN
TRANSGRESSIONS

PAGE 87
Sudoku X

5	9	4	2	3	1	6	7	8
8	2	1	7	9	6	4	5	3
6	7	3	8	5	4	2	1	9
9	5	6	1	7	3	8	4	2
1	4	2	5	6	8	9	3	7
3	8	7	4	2	9	1	6	5
4	3	9	6	8	5	7	2	1
2	1	5	9	4	7	3	8	6
7	6	8	3	1	2	5	9	4

BLOCK ANAGRAM
DERMATOLOGIST

PAGE 88
On an Even Keel

PAGE 89
BrainSnack®—
Web of Intrigue

Zone 6. Moving inward to the center of the web, there are two blue zones between each yellow zone.

QUICK CROSSWORD

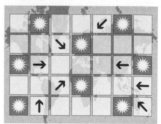

PAGE 90
Sunny Weather

TRIANAGRAM
DETERS, RESTED

PAGE 91
Suit Cases

P	R	E	S		B	A	S	K		R	I	D	E	S
A	E	R	O		O	B	I	E		E	M	I	L	E
S	P	A	D	E	W	O	R	K		T	O	A	S	T
T	O	T	A	L	L	Y		E	N	I	G	M	A	S
	P	O	I				A	R	E	O				
E	C	H	O	I	N	G		B	R	E	N	N	E	R
D	E	E	P		G	L	O	R	Y		E	D	D	Y
U	T	A			E	R	A			L	I	D		
C	U	R	B		C	A	R	G	O		N	I	N	E
E	S	T	E	F	A	N		S	C	H	O	L	A	R
		T	E	E	N				T	U	X			
A	T	H	L	E	T	E		L	O	G	I	C	A	L
P	E	R	I	L		C	L	U	B	H	O	U	S	E
S	A	O	N	E		R	E	N	E		U	L	E	E
E	M	B	E	R		U	S	E	R		S	T	A	R

PAGE 92
Kakuro

2	1	3		6	7	8	4	9
1	3	2		4	1		1	7
	4	1	9	8		3	9	8
3	5		7	5	4	2	8	
9	2	3	1		8	1	7	6
5		8	5	9	6		5	1
8	6	7		8	2	1		5
6	2			1	4	2	3	
7	8	5	6		8	1	9	

DOUBLETALK
CALENDAR/CALENDER

PAGE 93
Sudoku Twin

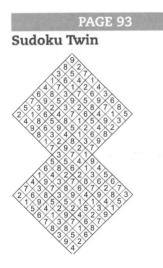

TRIANAGRAM
CHASER, SEARCH

PAGE 94
BrainSnack®—Beach Days

343°. 28° is always added to the degrees of the angle. 45° + 28° = 73°; 90° + 28° = 118; 225° + 28° = 253°; and the question mark is at 315° + 28° = 343°.

CHANGELINGS

B R A I N S T O R M
P E R S U A S I V E
A G R E E M E N T S

PAGE 95
The Elements

R	O	T	C		D	R	A	G	O		L	U	L	L
O	R	E	O		E	E	L	E	R		E	P	E	E
B	A	L	L	O	F	F	I	R	E		B	I	N	D
S	L	E	E	V	E	S		M	I	R	A	N	D	A
			M	E	N			L	I	N	T			
E	D	W	A	R	D	S		A	L	C	O	H	O	L
J	O	H	N		S	A	S	S	Y		N	E	V	E
E	N	O				F	I	T			A	I	G	
C	O	L	E		F	E	R	A	L		R	I	N	G
T	R	E	L	L	I	S		R	E	V	E	R	E	S
		E	L	A	N			V	I	P				
P	R	A	I	R	I	E		B	E	E	L	I	N	E
O	A	R	S		C	L	E	A	R	W	A	T	E	R
O	T	T	O		K	I	N	T	E		C	E	L	T
H	A	H	N		Y	E	A	S	T		E	R	L	E

PAGE 96
Construction

The construction industry is an economic sector that focuses on making homes and other structures.

DELETE ONE
Delete F and find CONSIDERATE

PAGE 97
Hourglass

(1) admires, (2) dreams,
(3) smear, (4) same, (5) sale,
(6) false, (7) flames, (8) females

UNCANNY TURN
THE GOOD SAMARITAN

PAGE 98
Hannah and Her Sisters

B	O	L	A		S	N	O	O	P		M	A	R	A
R	E	I	N		P	E	T	R	I		A	N	O	N
A	N	N	A	S	E	W	E	L	L		G	N	A	T
C	O	N	T	A	C	T		E	S	T	E	E	M	S
	O	U	T				N	I	N	A				
S	M	A	L	L	E	R		C	E	N	T	R	A	L
C	O	N	E		R	U	M	O	R		A	C	R	E
U	R	N			P	A	C			H	E	N		
D	A	I	S		A	E	S	O	P		D	E	N	T
O	N	E	T	I	M	E		A	I	R	B	R	T	O
		P	O	S	H			A	O	L				
S	H	O	R	T	E	N		E	N	L	A	R	G	E
T	A	T	I		R	A	G	G	E	D	Y	A	N	N
E	T	T	E		S	T	O	A	T		E	V	A	N
M	E	S	S		T	O	O	N	S		D	E	W	S

PAGE 99
Keep Going

FRIENDS?
Each can have the prefix CALL- to form a new word.

PAGE 100
Sport Maze

ONE LETTER LESS OR MORE

IGNORANCE

PAGE 101
Postgame Show

S	T	E	P	S		J	A	M	B		S	T	A	B
C	A	R	L	O		U	S	E	R		C	U	R	E
A	V	I	A	N		S	T	L	O		E	R	T	E
T	I	C	T	A	C	T	O	E	W	I	N	N	E	R
		E	R	R			E	N	N	A				
R	U	G	S		A	L	B		S	H	R	O	U	D
O	N	E		V	I	O	L	A		A	I	S	L	E
T	H	E	B	I	G	G	E	S	T	L	O	S	E	R
C	A	S	I	O		E	S	T	E	E		I	N	A
S	T	E	L	L	A		T	A	R		J	E	T	T
			L	I	S	P		R	E	O				
N	O	W	I	N	S	I	T	U	A	T	I	O	N	S
A	G	I	O		E	X	I	T		U	N	T	I	E
T	E	R	N		T	I	N	A		D	E	I	C	E
S	E	E	S		S	E	T	H		E	D	S	E	L

PAGE 102
BrainSnack®—Drink Up!

2.43. From left to right, the price of the next beer equals the price of the previous beer minus the sum of the former's digit total. 3.00 - 0.03 = 2.97 - 0.18 = 2.79 - 0.18 = 2.61 - 0.09 = 2.52 - 0.09 = 2.43.

LETTER LINE

RECAPTURED; CAPERED, TERRACED, RETRACED, TRUE, ERUPT

PAGE 103
Word Sudoku

P	L	Z	D	I	N	A	E	Q
E	I	Q	P	Z	A	L	D	N
A	D	N	L	E	Q	Z	P	I
D	A	L	E	Q	Z	N	I	P
Q	P	I	N	A	L	E	Z	D
N	Z	E	I	D	P	Q	A	L
I	Q	D	A	L	E	P	N	Z
Z	E	P	Q	N	D	I	L	A
L	N	A	Z	P	I	D	Q	E

UNCANNY TURN

THE DORMITORY

PAGE 104
End Rhyme

A	T	O	M		T	R	U	M	P		H	A	L	L
L	O	G	O		R	I	V	E	R		E	Z	I	O
T	O	R	N	R	O	T	A	T	O	R	C	U	F	F
O	N	E	T	I	M	E		E	P	A	U	L	E	T
			R	E	P		O	R	B					
R	A	V	E	L	E	D		A	S	I	A	T	I	C
A	N	O	A		R	I	S	E	N		O	N	A	
B	I	L	L	Y	G	O	A	T	S	G	R	U	F	F
B	O	G		I	R	I	N	A		O	S	E	E	
I	N	A	S	P	O	T		R	A	I	L	E	R	S
	C	P	U				M	A	E					
A	R	G	U	I	N	G		R	U	M	P	L	E	S
C	A	L	L	E	D	O	N	E	S	B	L	U	F	F
E	V	I	L		E	R	O	S	E		A	C	O	P
D	E	B	S		R	E	N	T	S		Y	A	R	D

PAGE 105
Sudoku

1	9	6	2	8	4	7	3	5
5	2	3	9	7	6	8	1	4
8	7	4	5	3	1	2	9	6
3	8	1	4	9	2	6	5	7
9	6	7	8	5	3	4	2	1
4	5	2	6	1	7	9	8	3
2	1	8	7	4	5	3	6	9
7	3	9	1	6	8	5	4	2
6	4	5	3	2	9	1	7	8

SYMBOL SUMS

7 x 8 + 8 ÷ 16 = 4

PAGE 106
Word Ladder

thin, inch, rich, hair, rain, barn

poker, power, owner, snore, horse, share, shark

FRIENDS?

Each can have the suffix -BOX to form a new word.

PAGE 107
Divine Nature

S	H	A	H		M	A	S	S	E		B	A	S	T
L	E	V	Y		A	L	L	A	Y		E	D	I	E
A	R	E	A		C	L	A	R	E		C	O	D	A
M	E	R	C	U	R	Y	V	I	L	L	A	G	E	R
	I	T	O			I	L	L						
R	E	D	N	E	S	S		E	N	A	M	E	L	S
E	X	I	T		P	A	T	E	N		W	E	T	
M	I	G	H	T	Y	A	P	H	R	O	D	I	T	E
A	L	I		R	A	T	T	Y		E	N	O	L	
P	E	T	N	A	M	E		L	A	S	A	G	N	A
		A	I	M			R	O	T					
J	U	P	I	T	E	R	S	Y	M	P	H	O	N	Y
O	R	A	L		R	O	W	E	L		B	R	A	E
E	D	G	E		E	L	A	T	E		E	Z	R	A
S	U	E	D		D	E	B	I	T		D	O	C	S

PAGE 108
Futoshiki

5	2 > 1	4	3
2	5	3	1	4
4	1	5	3	2
3	4	2	5	1
1 < 3	4	2	5

LETTERBLOCKS

EXAMINE
PRESENT

PAGE 109

BrainSnack®—Sign of the Times

11. Working in columns, start with the top number and subtract the number below it and then subtract the third number and the result is the number on the bottom sign.

DOODLE PUZZLE

OnLine

PAGE 110

Textiles

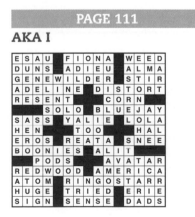

Textile means all that is woven, but the term also designates fabrics that are made in a different way.

DELETE ONE

Delete S and find TROUBLES

PAGE 111

AKA I

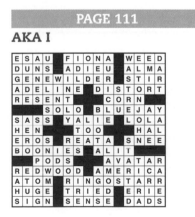

PAGE 112

Spot the Differences

DOUBLETALK

FIND/FINED

PAGE 113

Word Wheel

cue, cup, cut, due, put, cult, cute, dual, duel, duet, acute, adieu, adult, audit, cupid, cutie, lucid, tulip, utile, teacup, update, duplicate.

DOODLE PUZZLE

FaceBook

PAGE 114

AKA II

PAGE 115

BrainSnack®—Machine Code

L. The first robot starts with letter C and then every second letter from the alphabet up to K. The second robot uses the same system, but in reverse order from D to L.

WORD WALL

NONCONTROVERSIALLY, COMPREHENSIVELY, ATTRIBUTIONS, GOODNIGHT, BRIDGE, COG

PAGE 116

The Puzzled Librarian

1) *Rights of Man*
2) *The Art of War*
3) *On the Origin of Species*
4) *The Double Helix*
5) *The Selfish Gene*
6) *A Brief History of Time*
7) *Economy and Society*
8) *Black Lamb and Grey Falcon*
9) *The Prince*
10) *Leviathan*

DOODLE PUZZLE

NOnSmoker

PAGE 117

Before and After

PAGE 118
Binairo

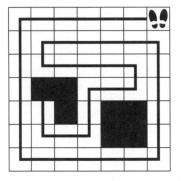

I	I	O	O	I	O	I	O	O	I	O	I
O	I	I	O	O	I	I	O	I	O	I	O
I	O	O	I	I	O	O	I	I	O	I	O
O	O	I	I	O	I	I	O	O	I	I	O
I	I	O	O	I	I	O	O	I	O	O	I
O	O	I	I	O	O	I	I	O	I	I	O
I	I	O	I	I	O	O	I	O	I	O	O
O	O	I	O	O	I	I	O	I	O	I	I
I	O	I	O	O	I	O	I	I	O	I	O
O	I	O	I	I	O	I	I	O	I	O	O
O	O	I	I	O	I	O	O	I	I	O	I
I	I	O	O	I	O	O	I	O	O	I	I

SYMBOL SUMS
21 - 8 x 6 ÷ 2 = 39

PAGE 119
Keep Going

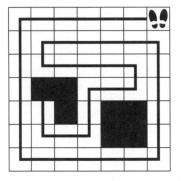

FRIENDS?
Each can have the suffix -LINE to form a new word.

PAGE 120
In the Vanguard

S	O	A	P		B	L	I	S	S		T	R	I	P
H	O	U	R		R	A	R	E	E		W	A	D	E
E	Z	R	A		A	N	A	R	M		O	V	E	N
L	E	A	D	I	N	G	Q	U	E	S	T	I	O	N
		O	D	D			M	L	I	I				
B	B	C		S	N	A	P		E	D	M	U	N	D
O	A	H	U		E	G	O	N		E	E	N	I	E
F	R	O	N	T	W	H	E	E	L	D	R	I	V	E
F	I	R	E	R		A	T	T	U		S	T	E	M
S	C	E	N	I	C		S	S	T	S		E	N	S
		G	A	L	A			H	A	H				
A	H	E	A	D	O	F	T	H	E	C	U	R	V	E
F	A	N	G		W	O	O	E	R		M	E	E	T
E	T	T	E		N	O	R	I	A		U	N	T	O
W	E	E	D		S	T	E	R	N		S	O	O	N

PAGE 121
Sport Maze

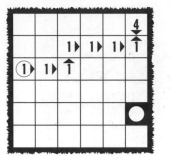

ONE LETTER LESS OR MORE
CASSEROLE

PAGE 122
BrainSnack®—Finger

Dot 5. All the other dots are in a straight line.

BLOCK ANAGRAM
GRAPHOLOGIST

PAGE 123
Night Lights

I	W	A	S	A		S	A	G	E		E	D	N	A
D	I	N	A	R		E	M	U	S		S	E	A	T
E	N	N	U	I		V	O	L	T		C	A	T	O
M	O	O	N	O	V	E	R	P	A	R	A	D	O	R
		A	S	I	N		S	T	O	L				
P	E	I		O	C	T	A		E	R	A	S	E	R
E	L	S	A		A	E	R	I		E	T	U	D	E
S	T	A	R	T	R	E	K	N	E	M	E	S	I	S
C	O	A	C	H		N	I	T	A		D	A	N	E
I	N	C	H	E	S		N	E	S	T		N	A	T
		E	R	I	C		L	E	A	S				
P	L	A	N	E	T	H	O	L	L	Y	W	O	O	D
R	I	D	E		C	U	B	E		L	I	N	G	O
A	D	A	M		O	T	I	C		O	P	A	L	S
M	A	R	Y		M	E	E	T		R	E	N	E	E

PAGE 124
Roman Empire

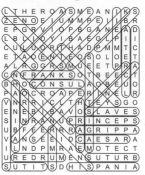

The Roman Empire probably became too large to be properly governed and protected.

DELETE ONE
Delete S and find A PATHOLOGIST

PAGE 125
Word Sudoku

M	B	R	J	O	A	S	G	N
A	O	S	N	B	G	R	J	M
J	G	N	M	R	S	B	A	O
S	R	A	O	N	M	J	B	G
N	J	O	A	G	B	M	S	R
G	M	B	S	J	R	O	N	A
O	N	M	G	S	J	A	R	B
B	S	G	R	A	O	N	M	J
R	A	J	B	M	N	G	O	S

UNCANNY TURN
THE SWORD OF DAMOCLES

PAGE 126
Sunny Weather

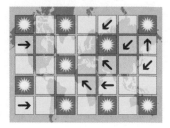

TRIANAGRAM
CREATED, REACTED

PAGE 127
Stripes

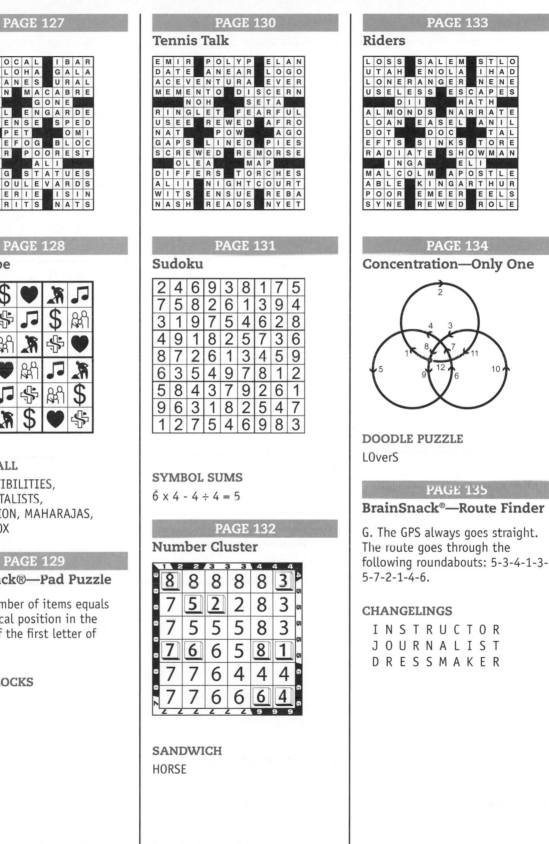

PAGE 128
Horoscope

WORD WALL

INCORRUPTIBILITIES,
FUNDAMENTALISTS,
ASSIMILATION, MAHARAJAS,
BUTTON, FOX

PAGE 129
BrainSnack®—Pad Puzzle

20. The number of items equals the numerical position in the alphabet of the first letter of the folder.

LETTERBLOCKS

ACRYLIC
FLANNEL

PAGE 130
Tennis Talk

PAGE 131
Sudoku

2	4	6	9	3	8	1	7	5
7	5	8	2	6	1	3	9	4
3	1	9	7	5	4	6	2	8
4	9	1	8	2	5	7	3	6
8	7	2	6	1	3	4	5	9
6	3	5	4	9	7	8	1	2
5	8	4	3	7	9	2	6	1
9	6	3	1	8	2	5	4	7
1	2	7	5	4	6	9	8	3

SYMBOL SUMS

6 x 4 - 4 ÷ 4 = 5

PAGE 132
Number Cluster

SANDWICH

HORSE

PAGE 133
Riders

PAGE 134
Concentration—Only One

DOODLE PUZZLE

LOverS

PAGE 135
BrainSnack®—Route Finder

G. The GPS always goes straight. The route goes through the following roundabouts: 5-3-4-1-3-5-7-2-1-4-6.

CHANGELINGS

INSTRUCTOR
JOURNALIST
DRESSMAKER

PAGE 136
On the Strip

PAGE 137
Volcanos

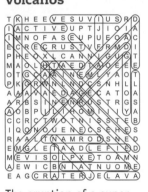

The eruption of a super volcano can have catastrophic consequences and lead to a new ice age.

DELETE ONE

Delete S and find LATIN AMERICA

PAGE 138
Sudoku X

7	3	5	9	2	4	6	1	8
8	9	6	3	1	5	2	4	7
1	2	4	6	7	8	5	3	9
4	7	8	5	9	3	1	2	6
9	5	2	4	6	1	8	7	3
3	6	1	7	8	2	4	9	5
5	8	9	1	4	7	3	6	2
6	1	3	2	5	9	7	8	4
2	4	7	8	3	6	9	5	1

BLOCK ANAGRAM

ORNITHOLOGIST

PAGE 139
Close Encounters

PAGE 140
Keep Going

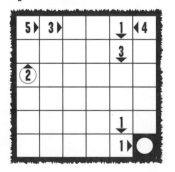

FRIENDS?

Each can have the suffix -WORD to form a new word.

PAGE 141
Sport Maze

ONE LETTER LESS OR MORE

LISTENING

PAGE 142
BrainSnack®—City Lights

14. Starting at skyscraper 1 there is always one more light burning.

LETTER LINE

READERSHIP; ADHERE, SHEARED, SPREADER, SHARED, RIPE

PAGE 143
Movie Quotes I

PAGE 144
Word Sudoku

B	I	O	T	L	P	J	A	N
N	A	J	B	O	I	T	P	L
P	T	L	A	N	J	O	B	I
T	O	P	L	I	A	N	J	B
L	J	B	N	P	T	A	I	O
I	N	A	J	B	O	L	T	P
A	P	N	O	T	B	I	L	J
O	B	T	I	J	L	P	N	A
J	L	I	P	A	N	B	O	T

UNCANNY TURN

SIBERIAN WEATHER

PAGE 145
Kakuro

DOUBLETALK
HOLED, HOLD

PAGE 146
Movie Quotes II

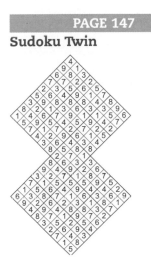

PAGE 147
Sudoku Twin

TRIANAGRAM
EASTERN, NEAREST

PAGE 148
BrainSnack®—Love All

2I. The ball always bounces as high as the distance it started from but veers toward the nearest vowel.

QUICK CROSSWORD

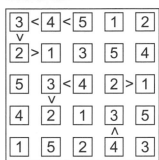

PAGE 149
Uniform Numbers

M A R V		A N D E S		S T L O

PAGE 150
Railways

Railways were developed in England at the beginning of the nineteenth century as a mining technique.

DELETE ONE
Delete S and get REDUCTION

PAGE 151
Futoshiki

LETTERBLOCKS
CHOLERA
MALARIA

PAGE 152
Castles

PAGE 153
Spot the Differences

DOUBLETALK
CHORD, CORD

PAGE 154

BrainSnack®—Chalkface

3. The average of the three numbers in each column is repeated under the line.

QUICK WORD SEARCH

```
G O L D S T O N E T I T K E T
S P H E N E P H R I T E D A J
Z A A M E T H Y S T E N R A G
I L N A I D I S B O L Y R E B
M O O N S T O N E T I L L E M
```

PAGE 155

Themeless

```
G I F T   L E F T   A S N E R
R O A R   E L L A   T H E M E
I N L A   B A I L   H O W I E
M A L C O L M M C D O W E L L
      T R A       I M I N
M A R O O N S   A V E N G E D
A M O R   C A R N E   G L U E
D A Y       M I V     A L I
A T O M   M O T I F   A N E T
M I R A G E S   L A U N D R Y
    B R A T       I L E
B R I T I S H C O L U M B I A
R E S I N   O A H U   O L A V
O N O N E   G R R R   N E M O
M O N A D   G L E E     E W A N
```

PAGE 156

Sunny Weather

TRIANAGRAM

LADIES, SAILED

PAGE 157

Binairo

```
I O I O I O I I O I O
O I O I I O I O O I I
I O O I O I O I I O I
O I I O I O I O I I O
O O I O I I O I O I I
I I O I O I I O I O O
I O I I O O I I O O I
O I I O I I O O I I O
I I O I O I O I I O O
O O I I O O I I O I I
I I O O I I O O I O I
```

SANDWICH

SHOP

PAGE 158

Sudoku

```
3 2 1 4 8 6 5 9 7
8 7 5 1 2 9 4 6 3
6 4 9 7 5 3 2 8 1
9 6 7 8 4 2 3 1 5
5 3 4 9 1 7 8 2 6
2 1 8 6 3 5 7 4 9
7 8 2 5 9 1 6 3 4
4 9 6 3 7 8 1 5 2
1 5 3 2 6 4 9 7 8
```

SYMBOL SUM

$19 - 3 \div 2 \times 3 = 24$

PAGE 159

Themeless

```
M A R C   C H I L E   D A T A
A B E L   H I D E S   E G A D
M A N A G E M E N T   L I R A
A T T U N E   S T A T I O N S
      S A R A   O T I C
P O W E R F U L   E N A C T S
E D H   L U R A Y   S T O I C
S E E S   L A M A S   E S T O
C O A L S   E E L E R   M A L
I N T A C T   R I C H M O N D
      M A R G   E R I E
W I N D M I L L   E N T A I L
E S A U   P U E R T O R I C O
P E N N   L E V E L   O D E R
T E A K   E D I F Y   S E R E
```

PAGE 160

Keep Going

FRIENDS?

Each can have the suffix -POT to form a new word.

PAGE 161

BrainSnack®—Life's a Beach

Pattern 2. The shapes on the first changing hut shift one step down and the bottom shape is placed on top, then they shift two steps down, then three and finally four steps. Since there are only four shapes, the pattern is the same as the previous one.

DOODLE PUZZLE

CubA

PAGE 162

Themeless

```
T A N G   L A N C E   M E G A
E L A L   I N C A S   E P I C
A E R O   A T O M S   W E N T
S C A R A B   S E E D L E S S
      I D I G   R N A
D A L A I L A M A   C A N O E
I D A   N I L E   R E C E S S
P O P E   T E A S E   C H I T
P R I S S Y   N I C K   R E E
Y E N T A   A A R O N B U R R
      D O C   S M E E
L A M B A S T E   M E A G E R
E V E L   A U R A E   R O T O
D I D O   G A M I N   S O U L
A V O W   E L A N D   E D I E
```

PAGE 163
Journalism

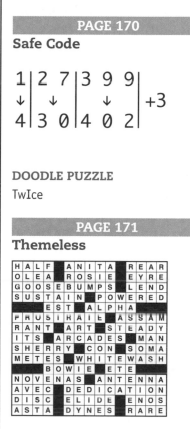

A journalistic message answers the questions who, what, where, when, why and how.

DELETE ONE
Delete S and find ALTITUDE

PAGE 164
Sport Maze

ONE LETTER LESS OR MORE
CORPORATE

PAGE 165
Themeless

PAGE 166
Word Sudoku

I	F	N	O	E	R	Y	T	A
R	T	A	I	Y	F	E	N	O
Y	O	E	N	T	A	R	I	F
E	Y	F	R	I	N	O	A	T
T	I	O	F	A	E	N	R	Y
A	N	R	Y	O	T	F	E	I
F	R	T	A	N	O	I	Y	E
N	E	Y	T	F	I	A	O	R
O	A	I	E	R	Y	T	F	N

UNCANNY TURN
HORS D'OEUVRES

PAGE 167
Cage the Animals

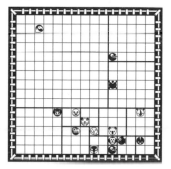

WORD WALL
UNDISCRIMINATINGLY, INSIGNIFICANTLY, ACCOMPLISHES, GALLERIES, BABOON, AIR

PAGE 168
Themeless

PAGE 169
BrainSnack®—Shapes

3A. Stack A belongs in location 3. Per stack the colors shift two places up and the shapes shift two places down.

BLOCK ANAGRAM
PHILOSOPHER

PAGE 170
Safe Code

$$\begin{array}{ccc|cc} 1 & 2\,7 & 3\,9\,9 & \\ \downarrow & \downarrow & \downarrow & +3 \\ 4 & 3\,0 & 4\,0\,2 & \end{array}$$

DOODLE PUZZLE
TwIce

PAGE 171
Themeless

PAGE 172
Word Pyramid
(1) to, (2) lot, (3) lost,
(4) stole, (5) hostel, (6) holster,
(7) ratholes

DOUBLE TALK
LAPS, LAPSE

PAGE 173
Hourglass

(1) obscure, (2) source, (3) curse, (4) user, (5) sure, (6) nurse, (7) insure, (8) sunrise

UNCANNY TURN
STUMBLE

PAGE 174
Monkey Business

1) *The Way Things Work*
2) *Open Wide: Tooth School Inside*
3) *How Much Is a Million?*
4) *How to Babysit an Orangutan*
5) *The Four Seasons: Uncovering Nature*

TRIANAGRAM
MELONS, SOLEMN

ANSWERS TO QUICK AND DO YOU KNOW

p 15: Jane Austen
p 17: Hamlet
p 19: Neil Diamond
p 21: Venezuela
p 23: Amman
p 25: *Get Shorty*
p 27: *Gladiator*
p 29: Gemini
p 31: Charles Dickens
p 33: Verona, Italy
p 35: Tenzing Norgay
p 37: *Mansfield Park* by Jane Austen
p 39: The five continents/regions of the world
p 41: Winged sandals
p 43: The Great Sphinx of Giza
p 45: A baker's fire
p 47: Ljubljana
p 49: Percy Bysshe Shelley
p 51: Jay
p 53: Riga
p 55: Moby-Dick
p 57: The Vatican (0.2 square miles)
p 59: Robert Burns
p 61: *I Me Mine*
p 63: Castries
p 65: 3
p 67: Metro
p 69: Donald Duck
p 71: Julie Newmar, Lee Meriwether and Eartha Kitt
p 73: *Leatherstocking Tales* by James Fenimore Cooper
p 75: William Faulkner
p 77: Perth
p 79: A goal, an assist and a fight in a hockey game
p 81: Praia
p 83: A ray
p 85: A 100-sided die invented by Lou Zocchi, sometimes called "Zocchi's golfball"
p 87: A corrective lens used to correct or enhance vision in only one eye
p 89: Zils
p 91: "Happy Birthday to You"

p 93: A tine
p 95: John Lennon and Paul McCartney
p 97: Spencer Tracy
p 99: 64
p 101: *Reservoir Dogs*
p 103: Sergio Leone
p 105: *On the Road* by Jack Kerouac
p 107: Audrey Hepburn
p 109: Germany
p 111: Wilma
p 113: Pilgrim
p 115: Louisa May Alcott
p 117: She induced an Egyptian cobra to bite her
p 119: Pete Seeger and Lee Hays
p 121: Marble
p 123: New Zealand
P 125: Chubby Checker
p 127: Henry David Thoreau
p 129: Helsinki
p 131: A British WWI single-seat biplane fighter
p 133: A cow kicked over a lantern in a barn
p 135: Eric Burdon
p 137: Czech Republic AND Slovakia
p 139: Ford Torino
p 141: Dashiell Hammett (*The Maltese Falcon*)
p 143: Frozen carbon dioxide
p 145: Raymond Chandler
p 147: Garbo
p 149: Nathaniel Hawthorne
p 151: Scottie
p 153: Howard Hawks
p 155: The Sparrow
p 157: Pelican
p 159: Alfred Hitchcock
p 161: Angie Dickinson
p 163: Lake Michigan
p 165: An Italian cycling event
p 167: Scott Joplin
p 169: Venice
p 171: The fog
p 173: The Duke of Windsor, who had abdicated as King Edward VIII of England